A SHORT HISTORY

OF

ROMAN LAW

BY

PAUL FRÉDÉRIC GIRARD

*Professor of Roman Law in the Faculty
of Law of the University of Paris*

BEING THE FIRST PART OF HIS

MANUEL ÉLÉMENTAIRE DE DROIT ROMAIN

TRANSLATED

(WITH THE CONSENT OF THE AUTHOR, AND WITH HIS SPECIAL
ADDITIONS AND CORRECTIONS)

BY

AUGUSTUS HENRY FRAZER LEFROY, M.A. (OXON.)

BARRISTER-AT-LAW

*Professor of Roman Law and General Jurisprudence
in the University of Toronto*

AND

JOHN HOME CAMERON, M.A.

Associate Professor of French in University College, Toronto

THE LAWBOOK EXCHANGE, LTD.
UNION, NEW JERSEY
2000

ISBN 1-58477-078-3

Printed in the United States of America
on Acid-Free Paper

The Lawbook Exchange, Ltd.
965 Jefferson Avenue
Union, New Jersey 07083-8605

*Please see catalogue at rear of this volume
or our website* http://www.lawbookexchange.com
for a selection of our other reprints.

Library of Congress Cataloging-in-Publication Data

Girard, Paul Frédéric, 1852-1926.
    [Manuel élémentaire de droit romain. English. Selections]
    A short history of Roman law / by Paul Frédéric Girard ; being the first part of his
Manuel élémentaire de droit romain ; translated (with the consent of the author, and with
his special additions and corrections) by Augustus Henry Frazer Lefroy and John Home Cameron.
      p. cm.
    Originally published: Hyperion reprint ed. Westport, Conn. : Hyperion Press, 1980.
    Includes bibliographical references and index.
    ISBN 1-58477-078-3 (cloth : acid-free paper)
    1. Roman law—History. I. Title.

KJA147.G5713 2000
340.5'4'09—dc21   99-087383

A SHORT HISTORY

OF

ROMAN LAW

BY

PAUL FRÉDÉRIC GIRARD

*Professor of Roman Law in the Faculty
of Law of the University of Paris*

BEING THE FIRST PART OF HIS

MANUEL ÉLÉMENTAIRE DE DROIT ROMAIN

TRANSLATED

(WITH THE CONSENT OF THE AUTHOR, AND WITH HIS SPECIAL
ADDITIONS AND CORRECTIONS)

BY

AUGUSTUS HENRY FRAZER LEFROY, M.A. (OXON.)

BARRISTER-AT-LAW

*Professor of Roman Law and General Jurisprudence
in the University of Toronto*

AND

JOHN HOME CAMERON, M.A.

Associate Professor of French in University College, Toronto

TORONTO
CANADA LAW BOOK COMPANY
1906

A SHORT HISTORY

OF

ROMAN LAW

TABLE OF CONTENTS.

CHAPTER III.

CHAPTER IV.

APPENDIX.

TRANSLATORS' NOTE.

The translators feel that there is little need of words of theirs to commend to students of Roman law any portion of the work of Professor Paul Frédéric Girard in that field. The present little volume is a translation of the preliminary chapter and the first book of his *Manuel élémentaire de droit romain*. The merits and the popularity of the *Manuel* are such that, though first published as recently as 1895, it has already passed through several editions; and the esteem in which M. Girard is held upon the continent of Europe, where naturally Roman law is studied more profoundly than in Great Britain or on this continent, is indicated by the fact that in 1903 the University of Heidelberg conferred upon him the high distinction of the degree of *Doctor utriusque juris, honoris causâ*.

Besides his *Manuel,* and besides numerous learned articles in various periodicals, M. Girard is the author of other well-known works upon Roman law; and the translators may refer especially to his "*Études historiques sur la formation du système de la garantie d'éviction en droit romain,*" his French translation of Mommsen's great work on Roman Public law, his *Textes de droit romain,* and his *Histoire de l'organisation judiciaire des Romains.*

As to the *Manuel élémentaire de droit romain*, Dr. Moyle, in his well-known edition of Justinian's Institutes, writing in 1903, refers to it as "a masterly treatise which it is much to be desired should have been translated into English."

The translators feel themselves proud to have been permitted to take at any rate the first step in that direction in the present volume. They are assured that, whatever may be the defects of their translation, the profundity and learning displayed in the book will commend it to those English-speaking students of Roman law who may not be sufficiently familiar with the French language to be able to read it with facility in the original; and the more so because, so far as the translators are aware, there is not at present published in English, and in separate form, any short history of Roman law. Muirhead's well-known History of Roman Private law is on a somewhat extensive scale, and scarcely suited for students to begin upon; while, though there are excellent historical introductions in Moyle's Justinian's Institutes, and in Sohm's Institutes of Roman Law, so well translated by Ledlie, they are not published separately. The translators believe, therefore, that this little volume will supply a very real want, and are glad to be able to add that M. Girard has made, specially for it, such additions and corrections as he has deemed to be needed to supplement the text of the last edition of his book; and has also kindly answered numerous questions submitted to him by the translators during the progress of their work.

In an appendix there has been added a translation of the *Bibliographie générale* with which M. Girard prefaces his *Manuel,* and which the translators feel confident will be deemed of interest and value, if for no other reason, because it will serve to make English students of Roman law realize the amount of learning and research which has been expended on the subject. It is believed that nowhere else can there be found so complete a guide to the foreign literature of Roman law. In this General Bibliography all contractions will be found explained.

It remains to state that the translators have deemed it best, after much consideration, to leave M. Girard's citations of works of other authors precisely as he has them, although, as is natural, some of the references are to French translations. They have, however, endeavoured, in all cases, to give the title of the original work in the General Bibliography.

A. H. F. L.
J. H. C.

PRELIMINARY CHAPTER.

ROMAN LAW—DEFINITIONS—DIVISIONS—INTEREST OF ITS STUDY—PLAN.

Law (*jus*) is, taking the word in its most positive and most technical meaning, the totality of the rules imposed by external compulsion to regulate the relations of men among themselves(*a*). The Romans were earlier than many other people in arriving at the point of distinguishing between it and religious rules, which have reference to the relations of men with their gods (*fas*)(*b*), and they saw just as clearly the line of demarcation which separates it from morality, the rules of which, considered as not affecting the public interest, are obligatory only in the realm of conscience, and may be violated without penal consequences(*c*). However, the distinction between

(*a*) This would seem to be the etymological meaning of the word *jus*, if one recognizes in it the expression of an idea of bond, with an etymology suggested by Pott and acquiesced in by Ihering, *Espr. du Dr. rom.*, 1, p. 119. But see for a different view Bréal, *N. R. hist.*, 1883, p. 605, and Schmidt, quoted by Mommsen, *Dr. publ.*, 6, 1, p. 352, n. 4. Cf. on the meaning of the associated word *lex*, the last named author, 6, 1, p. 351, n. 2, and for a contrary view, Bréal, p. 610.

(*b*) Not only is *fas* opposed to *jus* regarded theoretically, but, as matter of practice, the infractions of *fas* are not as a rule repressed by public authority. See on religious offences, Mommsen, *Dr. publ.*, 3, p. 56 *et seq.; Strafrecht*, p. 36 *et seq.*

(*c*) Paul, *D.*, 50, 17, *De r. j.*, 144: *Non omne quod licet honestum est.*

law and morality, at all times a delicate one to make in
theory, must have been marked in practice so much the
less precisely during early days at Rome, because the
law was then more exclusively customary, and there
must, even among the Romans, of necessity have been
an intermixture of law and religion, as long as political
and religious powers remained united in the same.hands.

Beyond doubt, the traditional influence of the past
is largely the explanation of the almost constant con-
fusion of the three domains shewn in the definitions and
general precepts which the later jurists habitually
made the preamble of their expositions of judicial science:—their enumeration of the precepts of the law, beginning with the duty of living honestly; their definition
of the law itself as the art of the good and the equitable;
and their definition of the science of the law as embracing at the same time things divine and human(d). We
cannot afford to remain ignorant of these formulas, which
have become proverbial; but perhaps their principal
merit is that they remind us how gradually the Romans

(d) Precepts of the law, Ulpian, D.. 1, 1, De j. et j., 10,
1=Inst., 1, 1, De j. et j., 3: Juris praecepta sunt haec; honeste
vivere, alterum non laedere, suum cuique tribuere. Definition of
law, Celsus cited by Ulpian, D., h.t., 1, pr.: Jus est ars aequi et
boni. Definition of the science of law, Ulpian. D., h.t., 10, 2=Inst.,
h.t., 1: Juris prudentia est divinarum atque humanarum rerum
notitia, justi atque injusti scientia. The definition of justice,
Ulpian, D., h.t., 10, pr.=Inst., h.t., pr.: Justitia est constans et
perpetua voluntas jus suum cuique tribuendi is the only one
quite free from these alloys.

themselves felt their way to the scientific notion of a law independent of religion and distinct from morality. I content myself with mentioning them without attributing to them a value which they do not possess.

The same compilations which have handed down to us this store of definitions and maxims, have preserved for us several divisions of the subject-matters of law which it is still more important to know. The principal ones are the division into *jus civile, jus gentium,* and *jus naturale;* that into written law and unwritten law; and that into public and private law.

The *jus civile* is that which is peculiar to each State, and which only applies to its own citizens. At Rome it is the law of which Roman citizens alone may avail themselves(*e*).· The *jus gentium* is, in the most precise sense, the law which is applicable, in the Roman State, alike to citizens and strangers; some see in it also, in a vaguer sense, law which, being found to be identical among all peoples, must consequently be common to all men(*f*). As to the third term (*jus naturae, natu-*

(*e*) *Gaius,* 1, 1=*Inst.,* 1, 2, *De j. nat. et gent.,* 1: *Quod quisque populus ipse sibi jus constituit, id ipsius proprium est civitatis, vocaturque jus civile, quasi jus proprium civitatis.* See for another more restricted sense of the term *jus civile, infra,* p. 90, n. y.

(*f*) *Gaius,* 1, 1=*Inst.,* 1, 2, *De j. nat. et gent.,* 1: *Quod vero naturalis ratio inter omnes homines constituit, id apud omnes populos peraeque custoditur vocaturque jus gentium.* Cf. Cicero, *De. Off.,* 3, 5, 23. On the other hand it is to the *jus gentium* in the technical sense that the distinction relates which is there quoted, 3, 17, 69, as drawn by the *majores between* the *jus civile* and the *jus gentium.*

rale), added by certain writers only, this is, according to some, an ideal law, somewhat akin to the law common to all men, elsewhere designated by the name of the *jus gentium*(*g*) ; according to others, a law which they take to be common to all living beings, just as the *jus gentium* is to all men, and the *jus civile* to all citizens(*h*). In its most scientific and simplest form, this division, confined to its two first terms, corresponds to the distinction between the most ancient rules, made for citizens alone, and the rules, more recent in my opinion, afterwards made for the relations between citizens and strangers admitted to the benefit of the protection of the Roman laws(*i*).

(*g*) Cicero, *De Leg.*, 2, 4, 8, *Inst.*, 1, 2, *De j. nat.* 11, etc.

(*h*) Ulpian, *D., h. t.* 1, 2=*Inst.*, 1, 2, *De j. nat., pr.: Jus' naturale est quod natura omnia animalia docuit: nam jus istud non humani generis proprium, sed omnium animalium. . commune est. Hinc descendit maris atque feminae conjunctio quam nos matrimonium appellamus, hinc liberorum procreatio, hinc educatio.* This idea of Ulpian's, which has been very ,roughly handled from the standpoint of theoretical law is, as Schulin remarks, *Lehrbuch*, p. 80, to be found already expressed in the writings of old Homer and the Greek philosophers, and is not devoid of meaning from the standpoint of the history of law. It is precisely by like reasoning that in our day the existence of marriage at the very beginning of human society is maintained by citing the habits of the higher animals. See for example Westermarck's *Origine du mariage dans l'espèce humaine*, 1895, pp. 10 *et seq.*, 40 *et seq.*

(*i*) See on this distinction, Krueger, *Sources*, §§ 6-17; Bruns-Lenel, *Gesch. und Quell.*, § 19; Pernice, *Z. S. St.*, 20, 1899, pp. 138-142. Enumerations of the rules of the *jus gentium* are given by Krueger, p. 56 *et seq.*, by Pernice, *Gesch. und Quell.* p. 102, and by Mommsen, *Dr. publ.*, 6, 2, p. 222, n. 1. In more than one in-

The distinction between the written law (*jus scriptum*) and the unwritten law (*jus non scriptum*) (*j*), depends upon the mode of formation, and not, as one might suppose, upon the material fact of the writing. The *jus scriptum* is that law which is produced by one of the public authorities invested with a legislative rôle, and which will, as a rule, be reduced to writing; the *jus non*

stance, the difficulty is to know whether the texts which attribute a rule to the *jus gentium* do so in the technical sense, meaning that it is one of which non-citizens may avail themselves, or in the vague sense, meaning that it exists everywhere. The Institutes, say, for example 1, 3, *De j. pers.*, 2, that slavery pertains to the *jus gentium*, while there seems scarcely any doubt that *dominica potestas* is peculiar to the citizens. There is, I believe, to say the least, much exaggeration in the theory according to which the *jus gentium* would comprise a sort of importation made at Rome, notably after the second Punic war, of the law of the most important non-Latin people with whom the Romans then came into relation, that is to say, the Hellenic populations of *Magna Graecia*, of Sicily, or of still more distant places (Gide, *Condition privée de la femme*, 2nd ed., 1885, p. 127 *et seq.*). As Pernice justly observes, the really Greek institutions of commercial law were grafted only with difficulty upon the institutions of the *jus gentium*, which had been already established before them, and independently of them: the *nauticum faenus* upon the *mutuum*, the *lex Rhodia de jactu* upon the law of letting, the *hypotheca*, if it comes from Greece, upon pledge. The institutions of the *jus gentium* developed rather in an independent manner within the Roman State in consequence of the juxta-position of Roman citizens and subject foreigners, especially, as I hold, after the *lex Aebutia*, and almost exclusively in the matter of property and personal rights (*patrimoine*).

(*j*) Ulpian, *D.*, 1, 1, *De j. et j.*, 6, 1=*Inst.*, 1, 2, *De j. nat.*, 3. Cf. A. Bernice, *Z.S. St.* 20, 1899, pp. 162-171.

scriptum is that which usage produces insensibly, and which consequently shapes itself without writing, but which naturally will not change its character because it may happen to be unofficially reduced to writing. However, the distinction has little practical interest.

A more interesting distinction, which recurs in modern law, and the credit for which belongs to the Roman jurists, is that between public law (*jus publicum*), regulating the organization of public authority, and the relations between individuals and the State, and private law (*jus privatum*), regulating the relations between individuals themselves(*k*). It is all the more indispensable to bear this division of the law in mind, because time-honoured usage confines the ordinary teaching of Roman law to the private law, uniting with it some few matters which a rigorous classification would nowadays attribute to public law (as, for example, the organization of the judiciary and civil procedure), and comprising in it also other matters which an evolution, already commenced at Rome, has transferred from private law to public law, namely, penal law and criminal procedure. These last belong to private law in so far as the punishment of the wrong done concerns the victim, but to public law when it concerns the State; and, consequently,

---

(*k*) Ulpian, *D., h. t.*, 1, 2=*Inst.*, 1, 1, *De j. et j.*, 4: *Hujus studii duae sunt positiones, publicum et privatum. Publicum jus est, quod ad statum rei Romanae spectat, privatum quod ad singulorum utilitatem pertinet.* Cf. A. Pernice, *Z. S. St.*, 19, 1898, p. 140 *et seq.*

they pertained to Roman private law in the degree in which they were contemplated at Rome from the former point of view.

But, its scope being thus determined, the study of Roman private law raises a question which the study of a system of law in active operation, pursued in view of an immediate practical application, would not raise—that of its utility(*l*). In answer to this question, three principal advantages are attributed to studies in Roman law with regard to which I feel all the more bound to express my views because these advantages seem to me to be of very unequal importance.

1. One ground on which Roman law has been much advocated, and on which it is still eagerly defended, is that of the direct professional utility which it is believed to have for lawyers, by reason of the materials which it is supposed to furnish for the practical understanding of modern laws. The present French Codes are the product of a fusion between the system of the *pays de droit écrit* which followed the Roman law, and that of the *pays de coutume,* in which the Roman law was at least admitted as supplementary law. The conclusion drawn is, that it is impossible to understand the latter well unless one has an adequate idea of the law from which they are

(*l*) See besides the principal treatises on Roman law, Rivier, preliminary lecture, in *Introduction,* p. 1 *et seq.,* and in the *Revue internationale de l'enseignement,* the Articles by Appleton, 1891, 1, p. 252, *et seq.,* Esmein, 1902, 2. p. 288 *et seq.,* and Jobbé-Duval, 1904. 1, p. 196 *et seq.*

derived through both channels(*m*). But I do not think this reason a decisive one. What it would lead one to study would not be the true Roman law, such as modern criticism aims at extracting from the totality of the extant documents; it would be the Roman law as it was understood by our older writers; for it is certain, for example, that when Pothier misunderstood the Roman doctrine, it was not the true doctrine of Rome, but the blunder of Pothier, which passed into the Code. A study conducted on this principle would be fertile in results as regards the understanding of the origins of our positive law; but it would have almost nothing in common with the scientific study of the Roman system of law.

2. It has been maintained more justifiably that the study of Roman law possesses a practical utility for modern jurists,—less direct, but nevertheless still strictly practical,—not as giving an immediate knowledge of existing laws, but because by perfecting the juridical intelligence, it is calculated to render possible a better comprehension of such laws, and of all laws whatsoever. The analysis of the discussions of Roman jurisconsults is, it is urged, an excellent school of juridical reasoning,

(*m*) This is the idea of the authors of the Code and of its first commentators (see the citations from the tribune Gary, from Portalis, and from Merlin, in Rivier, pp. 12 and 13), and it is also the same which at the beginning of the nineteenth century, caused Roman law to be placed in the curricula of legal instruction (law of 22 Ventôse an XII [March 15th, 1804], art. 2, establishing the teaching of Roman law in its relations to French law).

not only because of the mental vigour of the contro-
versialists, but for the very reason that the controversies
turn on points of law for the most part foreign to our
ordinary environment. The mind which has been broken
in to the handling of these dry argumentations will master with singular ease the relatively simple concrete difficulties of modern laws. Studies in Roman law have, it
is affirmed, in that respect, the same virtue that the study
of ancient languages has in all that at all deserves the
name of higher education. And certainly, these considerations are of great weight. There is no dialectical
exercise, no matter how barren it may be, which does
not sharpen and refine the understanding. And no law
is more fitted for such a work of intellectual training
than Roman law, which,—not at all because of any
miraculous genius of the jurists, but on account of various circumstances connected with its general history,
with the system of procedure of the Republic and of the
first centuries of the Empire, and with certain qualities
and certain defects of the Roman mind—proves to be
from the point of view of pure technical precision, the
most perfect monument of dialectic that one could find.

3. Nevertheless, it is not even there that in my view
the fundamental and decisive merit of the study of Roman law resides. It is above all an incomparable instrument of historical education. Laws differ at different times and in different places. In the matter of law,
as in the matter of art, of literature, and of religion,

each nation and each epoch has its own character; but the juridical level reached by a people at any moment of its existence is not, any more than its literary or artistic level, the effect of pure chance; it is the product of an historical development. Researches into the elements of this development, into the conditions under which juridical institutions grow up and change, constitute the most delicate and the highest branch of the jurist's sphere of work. And,—at any rate at the present time(*n*),—there is no system of law which affords a more favourable field for such researches than that of Rome. Roman law occupies, in this regard, a place apart, which it owes beyond question to its intrinsic doctrinal value; which it owes, also, to the abundance of documents of every kind, always permitting the investigation of it to be approached from some new side; and which it owes,

(*n*) Reason suggests that the same function would be fulfilled in a still more complete and higher manner by a universal history of comparative law. But, without speaking of the usefulness which would still belong, when compared with a general survey, necessarily somewhat summary, to the more complete examination of a determinate system of law belonging to the past, it must be admitted that such a general history of comparative law, (which would be of the highest interest, and which, I trust, will ultimately be realized,) does not as yet exist. The accomplishment of it presents enormous difficulties, and although it is being advanced nowadays with much more zeal, and by processes infinitely more scientific, than in the past, and although excellent materials have been collected, and certain first results have been placed beyond dispute, its completion will certainly require the efforts of generations of learned men.

further, to the enormous mass of work which has been
put into it during centuries by generations of commentators; but which it perhaps owes more than to all the
rest, to the length of the period over which it extends.
The history of Roman law runs from the foundation of
Rome, (which is placed by traditional chronology in the
eighth century before Christ), to the death of Justinian,
in the sixth century of the Christian era, and in this
interval it comprises an evolution which commences
almost at the threshold of social life, to end with the
decline of a worn-out civilization.   Thus we can nowhere
better observe how laws come to be, how they live, and
how they die.   There is no teaching better calculated to
prevent people looking upon the law of a given moment
of history as either an artificial and arbitrary accident at
the mercy of the caprices of the legislator (the mistake
of minds which are purely logical and ignorant of the
mechanism of social life), or (as is rather the mistake of
mere practitioners), as an immutable and eternal product.
There is no study more surely calculated to form, not
only professional men apt in the correct interpretation
of a concrete text, but men of science able to trace back
such a text to its first principle, and able to discern with
a sure eye the sound parts and the decaying elements of
a system of law, its guarantees of permanence and its
probabilities of change(*o*).

(*o*) I will not do more than mention, not as more doubtful, but as affecting a narrower circle of people, the necessity of an exact knowledge of Roman law for a perfect under-

This view of the subject determines the plan on which I shall explain the principles of Roman law. I shall not fail to notice, as the occasion offers, the links which connect it with our modern arrangements. I shall be careful not to neglect the doctrinal controversies of the jurists of the most brilliant period, not only because of the educational value which is attributed to the study of them, and which I myself recognize, but also because the minute analysis of the texts is the first essential condition of all serious historical research. But I shall bear in mind throughout that my principal aim is to retrace the very life of Roman institutions, without exclusively confining myself to any period, and without neglecting any.

And now as to the plan of my exposition. The shortest of Justinian's collections, the manual composed by his order for students under the traditional title of the Institutes, distributes its materials under a tripartite arrangement borrowed from Gaius, a contemporary of the Antonines, who had himself certainly found it in the writings of

standing: (1) of Roman history, with which more than with any other history, perhaps, law is constantly mixed up, not only as public law, but as private law; (2) of Latin literature, as well of the encyclopaedic authors (*polygraphes*), of such rhetoricians as Valerius-Maximus, Aulus-Gellius and Quintilian, or of poets such as Horace and Plautus, as of forensic orators such as Cicero, some of whose orations (for example, *Pro Roscio oomoedo, Pro Caecina, Pro Quinctio,*) turn entirely on points of private law, and have been sometimes carefully translated from the first line to the last by people who have not understood one word of the subjects of which they treat.

some older jurist(*p*). After having given some information about the sources, the definitions, and the divisions
of the law, he lays down as a principle that all the law
is reducible to the law of persons, the law of things, and
the law of actions(*q*) ; that is to say, that any right whatever pre-supposes three elements:—a person who is its
subject, who possesses it; a thing which is the object of it,
to which it relates; and an action which is its sanction, by
the aid of which it secures recognition and protection in
the event of its being contested. And consequently, he
studies successively, with more or less happy sub-divisions:—under the law of persons, the subjects of liberty,
citizenship, family, guardianship, and curatorship,—in
a word, what is now called the capacity for right, and
the capacity for action; under things, the different rights
of which they may be the object, to wit, real and personal
rights, interpolating rather awkwardly between the first
and the second the theory of universal transmission on
death, which applies equally to both; and under actions,
the methods of procedure by which one may urge the
different rights before the courts.

This division, which has been very widely accepted
in teaching and in theory, and which is still to be found

(*p*) The proof of this is that Gaius has already lost the key
to some details of the plan. See my *Textes*, p. 203. The edition
of the *Regulae Ulpiani* of Boecking, 1855, p. 192 *et seq.*, gives a
detailed table of this arrangement.

(*q*) Gaius, 1, 8=*Inst.*, 1, 2, *D. j. nat.*, 12: *Omne autem
jus quo utimur vel ad personas pertinet, vel ad res, vel ad
actiones.*

2—ROM. LAW.

in the laws of France, (where the Civil Code corresponds
to the law of persons and the law of things, and the Code
of Procedure to the law of actions), has been in our day
very sharply criticised, not only in its sub-divisions,
which cannot be justified, but in its very principle, and
has been abandoned for very much more scientific arrangements by several modern interpreters. Nevertheless, it is, I believe, of serious importance from an educational point of view, to preserve it in its ancient Roman
form.

I shall take it, then, as a basis, but only
as a basis, leaving out all the accessory inac-
curacies which are grafted upon it. Thus Justinian's plan places succession between real rights
and obligations, instead of analyzing all the elements of
property before passing to its transmission. Thus, also,
he places under the law of actions not only the rules of procedure properly so called, but the fundamental rules relating to the sanction of different rights, which would
have been more in place at the end of the theory of each
right. Thus, again, he presents the theory of civil death
produced by loss of freedom, of citizenship, or of position in the family, as an incident of guardianship, instead of treating it as completing the theory of citizenship, freedom, and the family. I shall disregard this
clumsy treatment, and follow throughout the method of
exposition which seems to me the most rational, but I
shall respect the principle of the classical divisions by
appropriating one book to the law of persons, one to the

law of property, and another to procedure. I shall, moreover, precede these three books by a preliminary book devoted to a general sketch of the history of Roman institutions in their relation to the formation of the private law. In truth, a part of the ideas which will be presented in this introduction—the views relating to what people in other days used to call by the name, now a little out of fashion, of the external history of Roman law; that is to say, relating to the different sources from which Roman law has issued at different epochs, and to the memorials produced by each—appertain, when strictly regarded, to distinct categories: the study of the organs by which law is generated belongs to public law, and that of the memorials belongs to what people call, nowadays, using the word 'source' in a different sense, by the name of the 'history of the sources.' But I do not believe that I need excuse myself by the precedent of the Institutes for giving here a general view. It would be, of course, impossible to study the private law without knowing in what documents it has come down to us; it would be almost as singular to study it without knowing the constitutional instruments by which it was created. Furthermore, I shall conceive my introduction in a sufficiently liberal spirit to comprehend in it some explanations about the workings of the organs of government, about the systems of procedure, and about the general evolution of law, which will afterwards assist us to a better insight into each separate institution, and enable us better to connect the parts with the whole.

HISTORICAL INTRODUCTION.

CHAPTER I.—KINGSHIP.

SECTION I.—THE KINGSHIP OF EARLY TIMES. THE PA-
TRICIAN CITY.

I.—*Institutions of the Royal Epoch*(*a*).

Roman history commences with the period of the
kings. Beyond question, the populations which founded
Rome already had behind them a lengthy past(*b*), and
their political form of government was, like their other
institutions, whether civil or religious, only the result
of a slow evolution(*c*). But the kingship phase is the

(*a*) Bruns-Lenel, *Gesch. und Quell.*, §§ 5-9; Girard, *Organisation judiciaire des Romains*, 1, 1901, pp. 1-45. Mommsen,
Hist. rom., book 1, chapters 4 and 5; Niese, *Abriss*, pp. 20-28
and the authors cited. Cf. Ed. Meyer, *Gesch. des Alterthums*,
2, 1893, pp. 510-526.

(*b*) Cf. von Ihering, *Les Indo-Européens avant l'histoire*,
1895; Helbig, *Die Italiker in der Poebene*, 1879 and the analysis
of G. Perrot, *Journ. des Savants*, 1880, pp. 434-442, 476-484, 530-
539; Ed. Meyer, *Gesch. des Alt.*, 2, p. 484, *et seq.*; Girard, *Org.,
jud*, 1, pp. 6-9.

(*c*) See on the political groupings of the Indo-European
populations before their separation, Schrader, *Sprachvergleichung
und Urgeschichte*, 2nd ed., 1890, pp. 568-585, and in particular
on the relations between the migration and the development of
royal power, Schrader, p. 583 and von Ihering, p. 368, *et seq.* Cf.
Schrader, *Reallexikon der indogermanischen Altertumskunde*, 1
Halbband, 1901.

most remote one to which the political history of Rome can be carried back. Even so, this history is in great part only a collection of legendary matter, or rather, indeed, of conscious falsifications, in which there is nothing true beyond a few proper names and a vague reminiscence of some concrete facts(d). There certainly was a regal period of Rome. The best proof of it lies in those institutions of the Republic which are only explicable as survivals,—such, for example, as the *rex sacrorum* and the *interrex*(e). But one can barely distinguish its most general characteristics underneath a corrupted and late tradition, made up to a large extent of conclusions drawn as to the past from the present.

Regal Rome appears to have been at first a somewhat humble collection of tillers of the soil and proprietors of flocks, grouped together at the extreme end of Latium, some few miles from the mouth of the Tiber, surrounding a fortified place of refuge (*Roma quadrata*), on a territory of only moderate extent and fertility. Its inhabitants were not distinguishable from the rest of the populations of Indo-European races settled in the regions bordering on the left bank of the Tiber. Many theories

(d) See Mommsen, *Hist. rom.*, book 2, chap. 9. Schwegler, *Römische Geschichte*, 1, 1853, has given a critical analysis in detail, still very useful, of the different materials of which the pretended history of the kingly epoch is composed. The dissertation of Mommsen on the legend of Remus, *Hermes* 16, 1881, pp. 1-23, shews, by a singularly striking example, the methods pursued by the first narrators of this story.

(e) Mommsen, *Dr. publ.*, 3, p. 2.

have been constructed, especially in former times, on the subject of the three tribes—*Titienses* or *Tities, Ramnes* or *Ramnenses,* and *Luceres(f)*,—the fusion of which constituted the city, by people who have striven to see in them certain opposed ethnical groups, and who have distributed among them in detail the paternity of the different institutions. But, although there may have been, at the time of its origin, or after the actual foundation, a certain incorporation of foreign elements, the Roman city presented from the first a very great degree of unity, and an aspect decidedly Latin. It did not differ sensibly from the other cities of Latium, either in respect to its economic level, or its private institutions, or its political form of government.

As to economic conditions, the earliest Romans lived principally by the cultivation of the soil and the raising of cattle. At the time of the foundation of their city they had passed the sociological phase, in which primitive man, possessing neither cultivated lands, nor domestic animals, has for almost his only means of subsistence the uncertain product of his hunting and fishing; they had

(f) The above is the official order of enumeration, and lends little support to the common notion, again revived in a new form by Schulin, *Lehrbuch,* §§ 3-5, according to which the *Ramnes,* the companions of Romulus, are said to have constituted the primitive nucleus to which the *Tities* of Tatius united themselves later, and then the *Luceres* conducted, it may be, by an Etruscan Lucumo. Cf. on the subject of this order, and on the more serious conjectures, Mommsen, *Dr. publ.,* 6, 1, p. 107, *et seq.*

also passed the phase subsequent to this, but equally prior to the separation of the different branches of the Indo-European family, in which, after domesticating their first animals, men lived the pastoral life(g). They practised the rude occupation of agriculturists, doubtless learnt after their ancestors, under the force of material needs, had effected their separation(h). It is infinitely more doubtful whether they had as yet any knowledge of individual property in the soil. Tradition represents each head of a family as having received from Romulus or Numa about two acres of land, on which he had his homestead and his orchard. But it is just this tradition which proves that alongside of this plot of land, insufficient to support a citizen and his family, the bulk not only of pasture land, but of arable land, must have been the common property of some larger group.

In respect to private life, the earliest Romans lived, as did many pastoral communities and some agricultural communities, under the patriarchal régime. At the head of each household, there was a patriarch, a *paterfamilias*, whose absolute authority, limited only by custom and opinion, extended equally over everything connected with the household, both human beings and things. He also alone represented the household to the outside world,

(g) See Schrader, *op. cit.*, p. 376 *et seq.*, and the résumé of S. Reinach, in Bertrand, *La Gaule avant les Gaulois*, 1891, p. 816.

(h) Schrader, pp. 407-433; S. Reinach, pp. 316-317; von Ihering, p. 22 *et seq.* The development of agriculture appears to be subsequent to the separation of the two great European and Asiatic branches of the Indo-European family.

whether in respect of the rare commercial transactions necessary at this period, when each family was, as a rule, sufficient unto itself, or in respect of the disputes provoked by the conduct of its members towards third parties, or by that of third parties towards them. He was in his household it has been said, in specific terms borrowed from the classifications of later ages, at the same time, the proprietor, the judge, and the priest. He was sole proprietor, not only of the products of the labour of his slaves, his wife, and his children, but strictly of everything, including his wife and his children, whom he could sell as he could his cattle and his slaves. He was the priest who took charge of the maintenance of the worship of the domestic hearth, of the sacrifices to ancestors. He was the judge, if not in civil matters,—in respect to which there were no separate rights, and, consequently, no possible legal proceedings between the persons composing the household,—yet at any rate in penal matters, where he could inflict all penalties even up to death, not only upon his slaves but upon his wife and children; though usage required him in the last two cases to take the advice of a council, composed of near kinsmen, but did not oblige him to follow it. In short, he possessed an absolute authority, identically the same, over everything which entered within the sphere of his action:—over his dead chattels, over his living chattels, such as domestic animals and slaves, over his wife, and over his children,—to whom must be added, in an enumeration which at all pretends to be complete, as being equally under his power and inseparable from his protection, his guests (*hospites*), (the members of foreign cities, temporarily at Rome, who could have no security except by placing themselves under the authority of a citizen, and who placed themselves under his at Rome, as he would place himself under theirs, if he went to their city)—and his clients (*clientes*), fugitives come to place themselves under his ægis, or slaves freed by him, who in those days would have as little security as the others, unless they remained under the *potestas* of a citizen.

To confine ourselves to slaves, wife, and children, there was, in later times, a vast difference between the power of a master over his slave,—which was itself distinguished from ownership over things (*dominium*), by the name of *dominica potestas*—and his power over his children (*patria potestas*), and that over his wife (*manus*). But originally these distinctions must have been less prominent, and have existed *de facto* only, during the life of the *paterfamilias*, whose power, in accordance with the most perfect form of the patriarchal régime, lasted for life at Rome.

The distinction would on the other hand become apparent at the death of the *paterfamilias*, when his children and his wife would become *sui juris*, and his male descendants themselves *patresfamilias*, whilst his slaves would only make a change of masters. But, as in other patriarchal societies, this dissolution of the *potestas* did not sever every kind of bond between those who had been subject to it. They remained agnatic relations (*agnati*) after the disappearance of the chief, which event gave rise to mutual rights of succession *inter se*, and to rights of guardianship in favour of males who had arrived at the age of manhood, over their young brothers, their sisters, and their mothers. This is that agnatic relationship which, at each generation, widened itself without breaking, so as to include all those who would have been under the power of one and the same ancestor had he been still living, that is to say, in a word, the relations through males.

Lastly, primitive Roman society,—like the Latin society of which it was a daughter, like the other Indo-European societies, and like other patriarchal societies of different origin,—presents to our notice another and final kind of private relationship, that of *gentilitas,* which is the relationship of a true or imaginary descent of a more remote description. Agnates were those who could prove, from generation to generation, their descent from a common ancestor, the *gentiles* those who, though unable to prove it, admitted this descent as attested by their community of name and of domestic cult. The *gens,* a natural product of the patriarchal régime, was a group of people who claimed descent from a common ancestor. In historical times, the things with which it was concerned were reduced to religious duties, and rights of guardianship and succession. Originally, its con-

cerns were doubtless more considerable, probably extend-
ing, for instance, to the enjoyment of the arable lands,
which may have been the collective property of each *gens*
before being subjected to individual proprietorship(*i*).

The political constitution of the royal epoch bears
an appearance of symmetry with this organization of
the family, which has long been noticed. It is reducible
to three elements, the equivalents of the first two of which
may be easily discerned in the family:—the king, the senate, and the comitia(*j*).

The king (*rex*)(*k*), whose function was certainly not
hereditary, but who, according to the annalists, was elected by the comitia upon the proposition of a senator, the
interrex (or rather, who was chosen by the *interrex* himself), was the head of the Roman community, very much
as the *paterfamilias* was the head of his household. He
had, like the latter, a power which was absolute and life-
long. Either personally or through his representatives,

(*i*) It is more doubtful whether the *gens* ever was recognized
within the Roman State as a political unit possessing an organ-
ized executive power and formally deliberating. See Mommsen,
Dr. publ., 6, 1, p. 17 *et seq.* and, to the opposite effect, Cuq,
Institutions, 1, p. 70 *et seq.*

(*j*) It would be indeed quite natural to see in this a case of
pure and simple borrowing from the patriarchal régime. But it
must be noted that royal authority, and still more the council of
elders, are met with in some communities which do not yet know
the patriarchal régime based upon the power of the father, and
where nevertheless private institutions have already sufficed to
furnish models for them.

(*k*) Mommsen, *Dr. publ.*, 3, p. 2 *et seq.*

he governed the city as the latter did his household. He was the chief of the citizens, particularly of the citizens under arms, of the army, as the father was the chief of his family. He was responsible for the State worship, as the other was for his family worship. Lastly, he was judge within the city, as the other within his household; and it may even be observed, that if his jurisdiction was at the same time civil and criminal, in his case, too, it was the criminal jurisdiction which appeared the more distinctly. For, in the only form of procedure apparently as old as this period, in which the matter in hand really was the settlement of a dispute or the decision of a lawsuit— in the procedure of the *sacramentum,*—a man could not get public authority seized of the matter, could not make it deal with the subject, except through a subterfuge, namely, by transferring the question to the region of penal law. The two parties took an oath of the truth of their pretensions, in such a way that there was necessarily on the one side or the other perjury,—a sin and, consequently, a delict, in this epoch when religion and law were not separated, and when, in order to know who had incurred the penalty, it was necessary for the king, head of religion as of criminal justice, to inquire who was right. In short, he had from a civil, religious, and military point of view, an authority much akin to that of the *paterfamilias,* and restricted, like the latter, mainly by custom.

The second element was the senate, corresponding to the council of kinsmen whose advice the father of a family was required to take in grave cases. In important affairs the king was not permitted to determine on a course of action without first asking the council of elders (the senate) for its advice, which council is sometimes said to have been composed originally of the chiefs of the different *gentes*, and was, as we are told from the first, formed by him, originally of 100, afterwards of 300 members. He was required to consult the senators, as the father of the family was to consult his kinsmen. But he was not bound, any more than the latter, to follow the advice given.

The parallel ceases with the third element of the constitution, the one which distinguishes the Roman kingship from those absolute kingships which are simple copies of the family power—the *comitia*, an assembly of the people consisting of the whole of its male members capable of bearing arms, without distinction of father and son, but exclusive of clients. The citizens (*populus Romanus, quirites*) were there divided into thirty *curiae*, probably on the basis of ten *curiae* per tribe (*Titienses, Ramnes, Luceres*) (*l*), but without the sub-division of the

(*l*) The thirty *curiae* appear indeed, as also the three tribunes, the three *tribuni militum*, the three *tribuni celerum*, the three *pontifices*, &c., to be a total number produced by the union of three communities, divided, according to the ancient Latin decimal system, into ten parts. A later doubling of the numbers of the military and religious official functionaries was probably the result of a new fusion, ordinarily attributed to Tarquin, of the city of the Palatine with the neighboring city of the Quirinal. See Mommsen, *Dr. publ.*, 6, 1, p. 124, and the references.

curia into ten *gentes* which some have deduced from a
mistaken interpretation of certain texts. The unit was
the *curia*, which was not only an electoral division, but
also a religious, military, and administrative division; and
which, moreover, does not seem to have been invented for
voting purposes (for in that case they would have given
the *curiae* an unequal number in order to secure the formation of a majority). The *comitia curiata* were convoked
by the king, within the walls of the city, and in general
at the spot called the *comitium*. At the time of voting,
the citizens separated into their respective *curiae*, where
they voted by heads, in order to give the suffrages of the
curia; then the individual votes of the different *curiae*
having been thus obtained, the total was counted in order to know in favour of which side the majority of the
curiae had pronounced. The *comitia* could only assemble
when convoked by the king, and they could only answer
"yes" or "no" to his interrogation, with no right of initiative or of amendment, and what is more, subject always to the ratification of the senate (*auctoritas patrum*). None the less they were the pregnant element in
the constitution. It was in them that the sovereignty already essentially resided. The king only consulted them
when he wished to do so, and only about what he chose;
but he could not make any change in institutions without their assent. Their acquiescence was requisite when-
ever a modification was to be made in the legal order of
things; and that is why they are found intervening in

the case of the reconstruction of the legal constitution of a family (*adrogatio*), of derogating from the legal order of succession (*testamentum calatis comitiis*), of exempting a condemned man from undergoing his punishment (*provocatio ad populum*), or of breaking a treaty by a declaration of war. The *comitia* could not take the initiative in any of these acts; but they alone had the power of authorizing them, the germ of their future right of command(*m*).

2. *Sources of the law. Leges regiae* (*n*).

Whence was the law of the regal epoch derived? The answer is still sometimes given, based upon modern notions, that it was derived from the vote of the *comitia curiata*. The law, it is said, had at this time, if not for its exclusive source, at any rate for a regular and copious source, the *leges curiatae*, voted by the people on the *rogatio regis*, and ratified by the *auctoritas patrum*, of which important remains have come down to us under the name of *leges regiae*, and of which a collection was made at the end of the kingly period, or at the commencement of the Republic, by some one named Papirius. But

(*m*) The evolution which led from the right of the comitia to have the matter submitted to them for their assent to their right of command is reflected in the parallel evolution of the meaning of the word *jubere* in the formula *velitis jubeatis, quirites,* which has equally passed from the meaning of accepting to that of ordaining. Cf. Mommsen, *Dr. publ.,* 6, 1, p. 355, n. 3, p. 353, note 1.

(*n*) Pomponius, *D.,* 1, 2, *De o.j.,* 2, 2, 36. See for the sources and references *Textes,* p. 3 *et seq.*

all three assertions are equally false: 1. The collection attributed to Papirius is probably an apocryphal publication of the end of the Republic, or of the time of Augustus. 2. The *leges,* which are supposed to have been transmitted to us by him (and in which, moreover, no one except the contemporary of Hadrian, Pompònius, sees *leges curiatae*), are in part, indeed principally are,—religious rules, which according to Roman ideas could not have been the object of a popular vote, a fact which is decisive in the case of all of them against the interpretation—merely conjectural at best—suggested by the modern meaning of the word *leges.* 3. Lastly, the best proof that the *comitia curiata* did not vote these laws regarding religion and penal matters,—that the *comitia curiata* never voted general abstract laws, but only the concrete deviations from the established order of things cited above,—lies in the evidence, perfectly uniform, according to which there was no written law before the Twelve Tables.

Up to that time, and consequently during the whole of the period under consideration, the law was exclusively unwritten, exclusively customary (*jus non scriptum, mos majorum*). As certain peoples, whose evolution has advanced but a little way still do, and as all who are now beyond this stage at first did, the Romans of the royal epoch lived under the rule of custom, of usages formed by an unconscious nameless process, which they no more thought of altering than they did the laws of nature. On this point, indeed, there is a thoroughly well established tradition,—so well established that Pomponius himself, who admits the existence of *leges curiatae* belonging to the royal epoch, is forced, in order to reconcile them with the tradition concerning the customary character of the law before the Twelve Tables, to suppose that they had been abrogated after the fall of the kingship.

SECTION II.—SERVIAN REFORM—THE PATRICIO-PLEBEIAN CITY.

Traditional history connects with the last legendary king but one, *i.e.*, Servius Tullius, a reform of the constitution about which a few words must be said before leaving the royal period.

1.—*The Servian Centuries(o).*

The primitive Roman people had for citizens only the members of the *gentes,* besides whom there were no other free men excepting their clients, who lived under their protection, but were not included, as they were, among the members of the *curiae.* Very soon a new element made its appearance in the city, formed of people who, while, on the one hand, they were not included in the old citi-

(o) Bruns-Lenel, *Gesch. und Quell.*, §§ 11, 12; Mommsen, *Dr. publ.*, 6, pp. 271, 305, 335, 435, 446, 180 *et seq.;* 4, p. 81 *et seq.* Cf. Huschke, *Die Verfassung des Servius Tullius,* 1838; K. J. Neumann, *Grundherrschaft der römischen Republik, Bauernbefreiung und Entstehung der servianischen Verfassung,* 1900.

3—ROM. LAW.

zen body, on the other hand, were not among the clients of its members, and who were called the plebeians (*plebeii*) in opposition to the old citizens, called the patricians (*patres, patricii*). The ancients supposed they had existed from the foundation of Rome. The most usual theory nowadays is that the *plebs* were formed gradually (under the influence of causes which are matter of dispute, and were, perhaps, manifold) according to one opinion, of captives not reduced into slavery, who having no patron, had only the king for their protector; according to others, of former clients, who no longer had any patron in consequence of the severance of the bond of clientship, as, for example, in consequence of the death of the patron without descendants. And, as we see to-day in commercial cities where an immigrant population confronts the old families with rapidly increasing numbers, the plebeians and clients, at probably rather an early date, reached the point where they constituted as against the *patres* (who alone had part in public life, and had become an aristocratic minority) an enormous majority, without civic rights or duties.

The reform attributed to Servius,—of which a description has been given us by the writers of the Republic, based on a picture of the Servian constitution drawn probably not earlier than the end of the fifth century (p),—

_____

(p) This results from the monetary system only introduced about A.U.C. 486, (B.C. 268) in which the figures are given to us particularly by Livy, 1, 43, and Dionysius, 4, 16. 17. See Mommsen, *Dr. publ.*, 6, 1, p. 279 *et seq.*

incorporated these new elements into the city, by granting them the right of vote, but probably mainly with the aim of subjecting them to taxation and to military service. It was, first and foremost, a re-arrangement of the general assessment of taxation and military service, which brought in its train the reform of the electoral system only by virtue of the connection, always recognized at Rome, between military service and the right of voting.

The Servian constitution had for its basis the tribes (*tribus, i.e.,* the territorial divisions, in which each individual was a property owner, and the number of which was increased with the development of private landed property), and the *census,* which determined the obligations of each man as a tax-payer and as a soldier, according to his fortune,—doubtless at first solely according to his landed property, and only changed much later to his property of every kind.

To confine ourselves to the military system, which was the origin of the voting system, the citizens, whether patricians or plebeians, were divided, according to the armament required of them in proportion to their fortune, into five classes,—each of which included an equal number of centuries of *juniores,* of less than forty-six years of age, liable to service in the field, and of centuries of *seniores,* of over forty-six years of age, liable to garrison service only,—and which comprised, as the first class, those who had, under the later valuation, at least 100,000 asses, but, probably, under the old valuation of land alone, at least twenty acres; as the second, those having three-quarters of this; as the third, those having one-half; as the fourth, those having one-quarter; as the fifth, those having about one-tenth, 11,000 asses, or two acres; while the rest of the population was not armed, but was bound to render auxiliary service.

The division into classes and into centuries being thus determined, the first class, the class *par excellence* (*q*), composed of men bound to general service, furnished forty centuries of *seniores* and forty of *juniores* = 80; the second, ten of *juniores*, ten of *seniores* = 20; the third, 10 + 10 = 20; the fourth, 10 + 10 = 20; the fifth, 15 + 15 = 30; and in addition, the army was completed by eighteen centuries of cavalry and five of musicians, working men, and complementary men (*accensi velati*). In all, 193 centuries made up the *exercitus Servianus*.

The voting was a sort of review, a sort of march-past of this army, which took place on the parade ground (the *Campus Martius*) where the centuries of foot soldiers voted successively by classes (after the centuries of cavalry, who opened the voting, just as they opened the battle), there being incorporated with the classes, in a somewhat obscure manner, not only the four centuries

---

(*q*) On the primary senses of the words *classis, classicus*, applied to the first class and its members in opposition to men of the other classes who were *infra classem*, see Mommsen, 6, 1, p. 297 *et seq.*

of musicians and workingmen, but those of the *accensi velati*, who voted with the last class. It was useless to continue calling over the classes when the majority of ninety-seven votes had been obtained; from which resulted, first, that the voting ended after the first class had been called over when the eighteen centuries of cavalry and the eighty centuries of the class voted in the same sense; next, that the last centuries scarcely ever voted. There is much more doubt as to the members of the first class having had a further advantage from the number of their centuries giving them, in the taking of the vote, a number of votes out of proportion to their share in the total population. That assumes that the owners of 20 acres who had 80 centuries could not have been four times more numerous than the owners of 10 acres, who had only 20. Now this impossibility has not been proved. It is just as conceivable that the number of members of each century was practically the same in all the classes, and that the number of centuries of owners of 20 acres corresponds to the proportion they formed of the total population before the disappearance of moderate fortunes and the appearance of large domains and pauperism. It is quite possible that this description has preserved to us the picture of a robust and healthy population of free peasants, at the same time agriculturists and soldiers, in which the majority still possessed (either by virtue of the recently developed rights of private property, or by virtue of the concessions of common lands, which had preceded them) the domain of about 20 acres considered necessary and sufficient for the subsistence of a single family. And this is also an indispensable supposition from a military point of view, for the Servian distribution was at first the actual order of the army. Nevertheless, the system does undoubtedly imply necessarily an inequality of effective fighting force between the centuries of the reserve and those of the active army, and consequently an electoral advantage for the members of the former,— mature men, less than 46 years of age, being, statistically, more numerous than those of over 46 years. But that was no military inconvenience, and was a favour to age which may be explained by political considerations.

2.—*Leges Centuriatae of the Royal epoch.*

The Servian centuries did not play a legislative rôle under the Kingship. There is in their case the same special reason for saying this as in the case of the *curiae*. Up to the Twelve Tables custom was the only law-maker. True it is that Dionysius(*r*) relates that Servius Tullius caused to be put to the vote of the people distributed by centuries fifty laws on contracts and delicts, but it also appears that the authority followed by Dionysius, had recourse, in order to reconcile this assertion with the

(*r*). Dionysius, 4, 10, 13, 25, 43; 5, 2. Cf. Krueger, *Sources,* p. 9.

tradition respecting law-making previously to the Twelve Tables, to the same expedient as Pomponius, *i.e.*, to the supposition of an abrogation by Tarquin. This is the best proof of the falsity of the assertion. At the same time, we have here an example of a rather common anticipation, which has led people to attribute to Servius Tullius, the good democratic king of the legend, certain institutions, introduced, as others hold, under the Republic. One may even doubt whether it is not due to a similar anticipation that Servius Tullius has been credited with the organization of the centuries, which is also said to have been abolished by Tarquin, but which may very well not have been established before the expulsion of the kings.

CHAPTER II.—THE REPUBLIC.

SECTION I.—FIRST BEGINNINGS. THE TWELVE TABLES(a).

I.—*Political Institutions.*

The foundation of the Republic is also placed in the legendary period, which can scarcely be said to end before the sack of Rome by the Gauls in A.U.C. 364 of the conventional chronology(b). There is no need, therefore, to dwell upon the stories which, agreeably to the never failing æsthetic sense of propriety of the ancients, connect the fall of the Kingship with the tyranny of the last Tarquin and the violation of Lucrece. The most that one can say with certainty is that the change worked in Roman institutions proceeded from a general movement, which took place at about the same epoch in nearly all the neighbouring states, and the tendency of which was

(a) Bruns-Lenel, *Gesch. und Quell.*, §§ 13-16; Mommsen, *Hist. rom.*, book 2, chapters 1 and 2.

(b) = B.C. 390. More precisely in B.C. 387-386. See *N. R. hist.*, 1902, p. 406, n. 1. The *annales maximi* of the pontiffs, which were almost the only historical source of any certainty for the early times, were without doubt preserved only from that date. See Cichorius, art. *Annales*, in Pauly-Wissowa, *Real-Encyclopädie* 1, p. 2252. Cf. Girard, *Org. jud.*, p. 46, n. 1, and *N. R. hist.*, 1902, pp. 398-408.

to substitute annual magistrates for the chiefs with life tenure who had existed until that time.

The transfer to two annual magistrates,—the consuls (*consules*) as they were called later,—of the political powers of the King, was in fact almost the only direct result of the fall of the Kingship. Of the royal power, only the religious portion was withheld. In order that the national gods might not withdraw from the kingless city that protection which they had accorded to the royal city, a religious king, without civil power (the *rex sacrorum*) was left in the ancient royal residence, (the *regia*). As to the priesthood, which up to that time had been nominated by the king, it was recruited thereafter by co-optation in the case of the great colleges (pontiffs, augurs, etc.), and by pontifical appointment for the inferior colleges and the vestals. But, in temporal matters, the consuls retained, in principle, during their year of office, all the powers of the king. During this year they were inviolable, as he had been during his life; they had, as he had had, the right of commanding the armies, of administering justice both civil and criminal, of convoking the *comitia* and the senate, and of nominating to the senate.

Nevertheless, this modification of the constitution, which has been defined as the mere introduction into it of a legal limitation (*i.e.*, of the definite term of office), was sufficiently important to be destined by virtue of its own force, as much as by the assistance of some accessory reforms, to displace in a short time the seat of power, and even to ameliorate sensibly the lot of the *plebs*, who, under the Servian institutions still remained excluded from all participation in effective authority,— from the magistracies and the senate, for example.

The constitution had the same elements as before: magistracy, senate, and *comitia*. But the position of each of them was altered.

The senate remained, indeed, a consultative body nominated by the consuls as it had been by the king; but it had, by reason of its stability, an influence over annual functionaries responsible on vacating office, which it by no means had over a life king. To protect themselves, the consuls adopted the practice of consulting it in advance, in regard to all important measures:—proposals of laws, treaties, financial administration, &c. It was a grave alteration, although only a *de facto* one.

The change was a *de jure* change for the *comitia*— for the ancient *comitia* by *curiae*, where the unit of vote was the *curia*, and in which the citizens voted simultaneously in the *comitium*; for the *comitia* by centuries, where the unit of voting was the century, and where men voted successively by classes in the *Campus Martius*; and for the new *comitia* by tribes, established between the foundation of the Republic and the Twelve Tables, where the unit of voting was the territorial tribe to which a man belonged, and in which the tribes voted simultaneously, in the forum. In addition to the legislative power, contained in germ in the concrete decisions come to by the *curiae*—in the matter of wills, and of adrogation, for example,—the *comitia* acquired the electoral power, (exercised by the centuries, who from the first nominated the consuls) and the judicial power, exercised in penal matters by the centuries or the tribes according to the gravity of the offence, by virtue of laws almost contemporaneous with the foundation of the Republic, which rendered obligatory in the case of certain penalties the allowance of the *provocatio ad populum*, previously left to the arbitrary will of the king.

As to the magistracy, on the contrary, the power of the consuls had limits of which that of the kings knew nothing:—the annual character of their functions, which allowed of their being prosecuted after their vacation of office; their duality, in consequence of which, while each of the two colleagues could act alone, the action of either might be stayed by the opposition of the other (*intercessio*) ; and, in addition, three restrictions, which are also represented as dating from the beginnings of the Republic, namely, the establishment of the quæstorship, the establishment of the right of appeal to the people in criminal matters, and the institution of *judices* in civil matters, each of which calls for a few words.

1. The right *provocare ad populum*, *i.e.*, the right of one condemned to appeal to the judiciary *comitia*, is represented as having been established in capital matters in A.U.C. 245 (B.C. 509) by a law of the first two consuls, and as having been afterwards extended to other serious

penalties. 2. As to the establishment of the quæstorship. the quæstors (who were at the time we are speaking of, appointed by the consuls) administered the treasury and criminal justice under delegation from the consuls, but under a delegation which was compulsory, which the consuls were forced to make, and which consequently deprived them of a portion of their authority. 3. It was the same in the matter of civil justice. Whilst, according to tradition, the king alone gave judgment at private trials, it is usual to attribute either to the founders of the Republic, or (by what we have seen to be a simple variation of the same notion) to Servius Tullius, the distinction between *jus* and *judicium*, that is to say, the obligation imposed upon the magistrate of not himself determining the issue joined by the ceremonial performed before him, but of remitting the determination of it to a *judex* chosen by the parties(c).

These immediate consequences of the foundation of the Republic refute the theory according to which the fall of the Kingship had been a defeat for the *plebs*, now bereft of the royal protection and placed at the mercy of their patrician oppressors. It is true that the establishment of the Republic opened to the *plebs* neither priesthoods, nor magistracies, nor, as I think, the senate. But there was here no aggravation of their lot; for it was just the same under the Kingship. And on the other

(c) See for the former version Cicero, *De Rep.*, 5, 2, 3, and for the latter Dionysius, 4, 25. 36; 10, I. Cf. Girard, *Org. jud.*, 1, pp. 77-82.

hand, since the *plebs* constituted the masses, it profited by all the restrictions imposed upon the omnipotence of the chiefs of the State, and notably by the reforms made in the matter of civil and criminal justice. More than that, the *plebs* achieved, in the period under consideration, a considerable direct advantage,—and, indeed, one not very reasonable,—namely, its recognition as a sort of State within the State, having magistracies and assemblies of its own, whose resolutions were applicable, up to a certain point, to all the citizens (*d*).

The plebeians secured, in consequence of a secession, and of a threat of separation, the creation of *tribuni plebis*, with the accompaniment of *aediles plebis*, and vested with the power of arresting by their *intercessio* all actions of magistrates within the boundaries of Rome and its environs. Over this territory, which constituted the civil in opposition to the military territory, the tribunes held, from a negative standpoint, an equivalent position to that of the consuls, upon whom they seem to have been modelled, in that they were, like the latter, annual; and, according to the dominant theory, in that they were at first, like the latter, two in number, of whom one had power to arrest the action of the other; and in that they were accompanied by the aediles, as the consuls were by the quæstors.

(*d*) See Mommsen, *Dr. publ.*, 6, 1, p. 100 *et seq.* Cf. Ed. Meyer, *Hermes*, 30, 1895, pp. 1-24; Girard, *Org. jud.*, 1, pp. 144-159.

But the tribunes did not confine themselves to this negative rôle. From A.U.C. 283 (B.C. 471), they were chosen in the assemblies of the *plebs* distributed by tribes, and they assumed the habit of convoking them from time to time in this fashion, in a species of mass-meeting,—called not *comitia*, but *concilium plebis*,—at which they put to the vote of the *plebs* resolutions of a character sometimes penal, sometimes legislative, and which, more and more approached those of the legislative and judiciary *comitia*. As to those of a penal character, they procured the passage of resolutions against patricians accused of violating the rights of the *plebs*, which logically ought not to have had any greater legal force than votes of censure passed by any private gathering, but which were apparently recognized as of binding efficacy even prior to the Twelve Tables. As to those of a legislative character, the assembly of the *plebs* voted, on their initiative, resolutions of a general kind which strictly ought not to have bound any but the members of the *plebs,* but which, from the period we are considering, seem to have been enforceable against all, provided the prior assent of the senate had first been obtained(*e*).

Lastly, to the initiative of the *plebs* and of its tribunes was due the most important event for the history of

(*e*) This seems to result both from what we know of the system re-established by Sulla at the time of his reactionary measures, (Appian *B.c.*, 1, 59; *lex Antonia de Termessibus, Textes,* p. 60), and from the circumstances under which the oldest *plebiscita* were voted.

Roman law of the first century of the Republic,—the codification of the customary law(f). The plebeians, it appears, accused the patricians of profiting, at their expense, from the uncertainty and obscurity inherent in

(f) See on the history of the Twelve Tables the original
authorities and the commentaries cited at page 9 of my *Textes*.
This history has, like all the accounts of very ancient events,
been disfigured by an accumulation of legends which it has been
the task of criticism to reject, and after the elimination of which,
it may be, nothing remains as absolutely established, except the
existence of Decemvirs, elected at the beginning of the fourth
century of Rome to compile the code which, under the name of
the law of the Twelve Tables, has been the basis of the whole
juridical evolution of Rome. But neither the fact of the codification nor the general authenticity of the text of the Code have
been subjects of any very noteworthy discussion until the last
few years, when the compilation designated by the ancients the
law of the Twelve Tables has been represented as in fact an
apochryphal work dating many centuries later than its supposed
date, first of all by Ettore Pais, *Storia di Roma*, L. 1, 1898, pp.
550-605; L. 2, 1899, pp. 546-573, 631-635, who has attributed it
to the famous secretary of Appius Claudius, aedile in the year
450 (p. 94) ; and then by Ed. Lambert, *N. R. hist.*, 1902, p. 147-
200; *R. gen.* 1902, pp. 385 *et seq.*, 481 *et seq.*, 1903, p. 15, *et seq.;*
Mélanges Appleton, 1903, pp. 503-626, who, at any rate in its
origin (cf. *Mélanges Appleton*, p. 518) has attributed it to
the jurisconsult of the second half of the sixth century, Sextus
Aelius Paetus (p. 96). I have cited, *N. R. hist.*, 1902, pp. 381-
436, the reasons, at the same time historical, philological, and
judicial, which appears to me to place it beyond all doubt that
we ought to attribute to the ten Commissioners of the beginning
of the fourth century the code which the grammarians and jurisconsults of the historical period had before their eyes, and on
the contents of which they have left us a mass of information
both precise and authentic.

all unwritten law. In order to remedy this, the tribune
Terentilius Arsa proposed in A.U.C. 292 (B.C. 462) the
appointment of a commission of five members charged
with the drawing up of a code according to which justice should be administered. The senate resisted, doubtless in the way above indicated, that is, by refusing its
preliminary assent to the proposal of Terentilius Arsa.
But the *plebs* held firm by re-appointing for eight years
the same tribunes, and after having tried to disarm them
by certain other concessions,—for example, by permitting
the *lex Icilia* of A.U.C. 297 (B.C. 457) concerning the
distribution of the public lands of the Aventine amongst
poor citizens,—the senate, in A.U.C. 300 (B.C. 454),
finally consented to a compromise. There was to be chosen
in the *comitia centuriata* a commission of ten members
for reducing the laws to writing,—the *decemviri legibus
scribendis*, who, indeed, according to the prevailing
opinion, might have been selected from among the plebeians, which would constitute this the first access of the
latter to the magistracies. In compensation, all powers
were to be concentrated in the hands of the decemvirs,
and the *plebs* consented to the suppression of the tribunate and to the suspension of the *provocatio*,—to the suspension of the *provocatio* until the end of the decemvi-
rate, to the suppression of the tribunate, possibly perma-
nently.

But the elections are not represented as having taken
place immediately. They had been preceded by the send-

ing to Greece,—or perhaps simply to *Magna Graecia,* in southern Italy,—of a commission of five members charged to study the Hellenic laws. It was only after the return of the commissioners, ten years after the proposition of Terentilius Arsa, in A.U.C. 302 (B.C. 452), that the decemvirs were appointed for the year 303 (B.C. 451). These decemvirs, all selected from among the patricians—of whom the best known is Appius Claudius—reduced to writing, during the first year, a certain number of laws which were voted by the centuries and displayed on ten tables of wood or of metal, close to the *comitium,* where justice was administered. The Code still appearing to be incomplete, new decemvirs were appointed at the end of A.U.C. 303, amongst whom, it is maintained, the *plebs* had for the first time some representatives, and who framed some new laws, but who aspired to perpetuate themselves in power, in which they are said to have remained even after the end of the year 304 and during the whole of the year 305. It was these second decemvirs, who, according to the legend, were overturned by the people under well-known circumstances, namely, the attempt made by Appius Claudius illegally to place the plebeian Virginia in the temporary possession of one of his confederates, under pretext of a dispute as to her freedom, followed by the death of Virginia at the hands of her father. After their overthrow their last laws were submitted to the *comitia centuriata* for their sanction, engraved upon two other tables, which constituted with the ten former ones the Twelve Tables (*duodecim tabulae, lex duodecim tabularum, lex decemviralis,* sometimes simply *lex*).

2.—*Sources of the Law.*

The period which extends from the establishment of the Republic to the Twelve Tables is the first in which we find a source of the law distinct from custom, distinct from the *jus non scriptum*. Now, moreover, we come upon the first source of the *jus scriptum*, the *lex*. We may cite as examples certain laws of the *comitia centuriata*, the *lex Valeria Horatia de provocatione,* the law of the Twelve Tables, and,—taking the word *lex* in its later broad sense, in which it includes even *plebiscita,*—certain *plebiscita,* as, for example, the Icilian law *de Aventino publicando*.

The law of the Twelve Tables(*g*), the only one of these laws upon which it is necessary to dwell in a treatise on private law, is the fundamental document of Roman law. In it all the prior juridical activity finds expression; and by it all the subsequent development has been con-

(*g*) See *Textes*, p. 9 *et seq.,* for a note concerning them and for the extant fragments. The indispensable work from the philological point of view to-day is that of Schoell, *Legis XII tabularum reliquiae,* 1866, certain readings in which have been modified by Mommsen, in Bruns, *Fontes.* The work published by Dirksen in 1824 is perhaps still worth consulting for the commentary. That of Voigt, *Die XII Tafeln,* 2 vols., 1883, comprises a restoration which it is quite impossible to accept, and a commentary which is extremely conjectural.

trolled. The formation of the Twelve Tables marks, it has been pointed out, a moment in the history of Roman law comparable to that which the committal to writing of the Homeric poems marks in the history of Greek literature.

The Twelve Tables did not long remain under the eyes of the Romans in their original form. The original tables cannot have survived the sack of Rome by the Gauls (p. 40, n. b.), in which they must have been burnt, if they were of wood, or carried away with the rest of the booty, if they were of bronze. They were afterwards reproduced, as were the other public documents, with essential fidelity, no doubt, but in a form already modernized; and a like process of modernization seems to have been repeated at several subsequent periods. In this form, which is not of any very precise date, they were the subject of numerous legal commentaries, of which the latest is that in six books written under the Antonines by Gaius; and they apparently remained publicly posted up until, at all events, the third century of our era. Nevertheless no copy of them, nor yet any commentary upon them, has come down to us in its entirety, and we are consequently obliged to rely for our knowledge of them on incidental citations,—which are, however, very numerous, and are found scattered throughout Roman literature. These citations do not permit of the actual form of them being restored at all perfectly; but, for all that, they are sufficiently explicit, and sufficiently numerous, to give us a clear knowledge of their subject-matter. They reveal to us very distinctly a rude and barbarous system of law, still strongly imbued with the characteristics of primitive legal systems, and probably not differing much from the law which had been in operation for centuries.

In fact, we must not conclude from the account of the sending of a commission to Greece, or from another story respecting the assistance given to the Decemvirs by the Greek emigrant Hermodorus, that the Twelve Tables were a copy, in any degree, of the Greek laws. The ancients indicate only two or three borrowed provisions, and those altogether secondary, while the others which certain modern authorities would add, are more than doubtful. Neither must it be supposed that the Decemvirs, who had received authority to reform the existing law, employed it to produce a work reasoned out philosophically, breaking away from tradition, and establishing political or civil equality. The Twelve Tables did not put an end to the exclusive right of the patricians to the magistracies, nor did they even permit marriage between patricians and plebeians. They may have contained some alleviations of the early harshness of the law,—for example, in the matter of family; and it is, also probably to the Decemvirs that we must attribute the introduction of money coined by the State, and the civil consequences which resulted from that. But the principal innovation, without doubt, lay in the mere fact of the formulation ot the law in writing,—in that substitution of a written law for a customary law which was the principal demand of the plebeians. This is indeed the best explanation of the limitations of the codification. Instead of embracing all the law, public and private, civil and religious, the Twelve Tables treat almost exclusively of civil law, of penal law, and of the procedure appertaining thereto. They scarcely contain anything else, except some provisions about funerals, and perhaps about the calendar, which was still important in reference to procedure.

To confine ourselves to the provisions relating to penal law, family, property and personal rights, and civil procedure,—the Twelve Tables, in penal matters, are concerned equally with public delicts, regarded as involving the State and repressed by it, and private delicts, regarded as exclusively injuring the individual, to whom alone it pertains to exact their repression. Public delicts, which, even at that early date, are not regarded exclusively as delicts against the State, but include, also, certain serious delicts against individuals,—as, for example, homicide,—are, when the penalty which they involve permits of *provocatio*, judged by the people—by the *comitia centuriata* in a capital matter, by the tribes in the case of the other penalties which permit of *provocatio*, that is to say, fines exceeding a certain amount. As to private delicts, the Twelve Tables enable us to catch a glimpse of a very instructive transitory phase in their evolution. In the case of some of them,—as, for example, of theft

detected in the act (*furtum manifestum*), and of injury
received by the breaking of a limb,—the individual
wronged has the right to take private vengeance with
impunity, as he doubtless always had in the earliest
times; he will not waive his private vengeance in return
for a ransom unless he chooses to do so, fixing the
amount of it to his own liking. On the other hand, in
most cases, public authority compels him to content himself with a ransom fixed by itself, with a compulsory
compromise. It transforms the individual's right of
vengeance into a claim for compensation.

The family of the Twelve Tables is throughout the patriarchal family based upon the *potestas*, in which there
is only one master, and only one proprietor, in the household; in which descent through males is alone recognized;
in which the wife is also under the power of the husband (or of the husband's father), by virtue of the *con-
ventio in manum*,—possibly always, but at any rate generally; and in which women cease to be subject to marital
or paternal power only to fall under the guardianship of
their kinsmen.

In the law of property and personal rights,—under
which ownership henceforth applies both to movables and
immovables, and obligations may arise not only from delicts, but also from contracts (*nexum, sponsio,*)—transactions are generally, and perhaps exclusively, regulated
by the system of formalism. To perform a valid juristic·
act, to dispose of one's property at death by will, to

alienate a slave *inter vivos*, or to make oneself a debtor
for a sum of money, the manifestation of one's will is
not sufficient. It is necessary, as under all primitive
systems of law, to have recourse to legal forms, to employ
gestures, and words fixed by law, which have the advantage of definitely manifesting, before his own eyes and
those of other people, what the actor is really doing, of
protecting him against surprise, and of facilitating proof,
and the equivalent of which, for this reason, we still find
to-day in the case of certain important transactions; yet
which were not invented on account of their practical
advantages, but were resorted to simply because men
had not yet, in those days, arrived at the idea that the
human will could by itself alone dispose of a right of
property, create an obligation, or produce an effect in
law. To attain these different results they employed
instruments which a process of development, requiring
separate study in each case, had caused to be recognized
as apt for that purpose.

The procedure which the Twelve Tables sanction, the
procedure of the *actiones legis,* is in like manner a procedure altogether archaic, rich in resemblance to the
procedure of Celtic law, to the Germanic procedure, to
the old French procedure, and to that of an infinite
number of groups at an early stage of evolution. It is
brutal and harsh. The claimant who wants the defendant to appear before the magistrate has the right to
drag him there by force; the defendant who does not

comply with the judgment may be put to death or sold
as a slave.   It is also rigorously formal.   In order to
join in a lawsuit it is indispensable for the parties to
perform the solemnities of a fixed ritual, to pronounce
certain sacramental words, in which it is forbidden to
them to make any change on pain of nullity. Lastly, it
shews another characteristic, often more overlooked, by
which the Twelve Tables mark a very noteworthy historical phase.   When we speak nowadays of the procedure by
which a person secures satisfaction of his right, we generally are thinking of a judiciary procedure where a
superior authority intervenes between those interested,
for the purpose of finding where the right is, and of se-
curing its execution.   But this presupposes the existence
of a judiciary power, of a public authority able to im-
pose its arbitrament upon the parties, and recognizing
its duty of giving them the benefit of it.   Now that
power did not always exist.   The starting point in
procedure was the right of doing oneself justice, just
as it was in penal law the right of vengeance.   The one
does not essentially differ from the other.   He who be-
lieves he has a right does not ask for justice; he takes it
himself, following, however, forms rigorously fixed by
usage, and running the risk of committing a delict if he
acts without right, or outside the forms.   There is a procedure, but there is not a legal process.   Now here again
the law of the Twelve Tables with its four *legis actiones—
sacramentum, judicis postulatio, manus injectio, pignoris*

capio (to which certain later laws added the *condictio*,) — marks a transition, and demonstrates very well how men passed from one system to the other, and how the new element, that of legal process, became grafted upon the ancient procedure without legal process.

The ancient system appears at first in full light in the *pignoris capio*, the seizure of a pledge, an archaic procedure, which at Rome is from the first a decaying one, which only continues to operate for certain creditors of a public and religious order, but which is found, with quite a different extension, in certain other systems of law, and of which the fundamental idea is forever springing up anew in the public mind. In order to bring pressure upon the will of the debtor, the creditor himself seizes, no matter where, without the concurrence of any authority, an object belonging to the debtor which he will only return to him when he is paid.

The *manus injectio* is a procedure in which the creditor solemnly seizes hold of his debtor in the presence of the magistrate, in order to take him home with him as a prisoner, and proceed later to his death or to his reduction into slavery, unless a third party (*vindex*) intervenes to oppose himself to this attachment of the person. It takes place before the magistrate. It may even give rise to legal process, if the third party intervenes; and consequently it is often looked upon as a legal process in the modern sense. In reality it is far from that. It approximates very nearly to the system under which there is a procedure without legal process, and a man takes justice for himself under certain legal forms; for the debtor cannot defend himself, neither—a point often misunderstood—when the *vindex* does intervene, does he defend him. He frees him by his intervention. But he is subject to penalty if he intervenes wrongfully. Thus the procedure of *manus injectio* is a procedure which does not result in any legal process, whether it comes to its normal termination or falls through,—save that there is a question for determination in the second case between its prime mover and the *vindex*, between the *manus injioiens* and the *manus depellens*. And it must not be objected that we have here a mode of execution which must have been preceded by a true legal process; for it seems probable that there had been a period during which *manus injectio*, together with *pignoris capio*, was the sole action of the law, when it provided a sanction for certain debts which gave rise to it of themselves,—for example, that arising out of *nexum*.

As to the procedure of the *sacramentum*, its precise office was to transform into debts upon which *manus injectio* might be based, certain debts which did not themselves support it. In this procedure again, the parties did not appear in direct fashion before the magistrate to have a difficulty settled. The claimant commenced by an affirmation of his right, which if it was not contested in the regular way, sufficed without legal process to render his claim susceptible of *manus injectio*. It was only on the negative response of the defendant that they proceeded to enter upon a legal process by an expedient already referred to (p. 28), namely, reciprocal oath, replaced later by a wager, giving rise to an inquiry, which at one time was carried on by the magistrate, but, after the establishment of the Republic, had to be remitted to a *judex*. After such enquiry, the claimant, if successful, would have, if the action was a personal one, the right of making *manus injectio*. But we see by what roundabout means legal process is here grafted on to procedure under which one takes justice for oneself without legal process.

The modern idea of legal process, of justice which one demands from a competent authority instead of taking it oneself, on the other hand, clearly makes itself manifest in the very name of the *judicis postulatio*, the demand from the magistrate for a *judex*, permitted for certain claims, and already recognized by the Twelve Tables,—which therefore afford, in the matter of procedure as in the matter of delicts, at the same time evidence of the ancient régime, and also of the new.

SECTION II.—THE HISTORICAL PERIOD.

(A.U.C. 305-727; B.C. 449-27).

The period which runs from the drawing up of the Twelve Tables to the establishment of the principate, is perhaps the most important period of Roman history, not only for the political history but for the history of private law. As regards political history, this is the period during which was accomplished, in domestic matters, the emancipation of the *plebs*, and in which, in foreign affairs, the Roman domination extended itself first over Italy, and afterwards over the greater part of the provinces. As regards the history of the law, this is the period when the more modern rules of the praetorian law and of the *jus gentium* began to confront the rules of the ancient *jus civile*, and in which, first, in the interpretations of the text of the Twelve Tables, and then by virtue of the larger powers given to the judiciary magistrates by the establishment of a new system of procedure, those principles were fixed, which the better known jurists of the Imperial epoch did but formulate and develope. I shall content myself here by summarily indicating the main springs of the constitutional mechanism, while dwelling principally upon the development of law and of the science of the law.

Political Institutions(a).

Political institutions continue to be connected with the three elements of the primitive constitution, the magistracy, the people, and the senate.

I. Magistracy. The change undergone by the magistracy is reducible, if details are excluded, to two

---

(a) Bruns-Lenel *Gesch. und Quell.*, §§ 20-22; Mommsen, *Hist. rom.*, book 2, chapter 3; book 3, chapter 11; book 4, chapter 2-4. 6. 9-11; book 5, chapter 11.

principal heads: (1) the opening of it to the plebeians;
(2) its division into distinct departments.

1. The patrician magistracies became accessible to the
plebeians. The Twelve Tables, while codifying the
pre-existing law, had not brought about equality for
the *plebs*, even from a private standpoint, that of
the authorisation of marriage between the two orders:
still less from a public standpoint, that of the throwing
open of the magistracies of the State. The prohibition .
in relation to marriage was removed very shortly afterwards, in A.U.C. 309 (B.C. 445), by a *plebiscitum*, no
doubt previously authorized by the senate, the *lex
Canuleia*. The achievement of political equality took
much longer and was more difficult; moreover, its history is so much intermingled with the movement towards
the multiplication of the magistracies that we must mark
separately the accession of the plebeians to each distinct
magistracy. And owing to this fact, also, the new magistracies,—for example, the prætorship and the curule
ædileship, created in A.U.C. 387 (B.C. 367) for civil
justice and the oversight of the streets and markets,—are
often represented, with some little exaggeration, as having been successively founded by the patricians in order
to retain in them the monopoly of certain attributes de-
tached from the pre-existing magistracies at the moment
when the plebeians entered upon the latter.

Notwithstanding all this, in the fifth century of Rome,
all the magistracies and the greater part of the priest-

hoods had become accessible to the plebeians; while, on the other hand, the tribunate and the plebeian ædileship still remained closed to the patricians. The triumph of the *plebs* was achieved in respect to the magistracies contemporaneously, as we shall see, with their triumph in respect to legislative power and the senatorial rights of their members. The ancient opposition no longer continued to exist between the two orders. It was replaced by a new social demarcation, by the formation of a new aristocracy, the *nobilitas*, the noblesse of the magistracies, composed of the ancient patrician families and those plebeians families who had amongst their ancestors a curule magistrate.

2. Perhaps partly as a consequence of the circumstances under which accession to the magistracies was achieved by the *plebs*, but beyond question principally by reason of the new needs produced by the growth of the State,—the character of the magistracy was changed. The magistracy lost its unitary and universal character to break up into a number of distinct jurisdictions. Instead of belonging in its entirety to a single magistrate (the king), or to two (the consuls) authority was distributed between numerous magistrates, each having in theory some of the special powers separated off from that general authority.

The consuls, indeed, kept the fundamental authority, that is to say,—in military affairs, the right of levying and commanding the troops; in civil affairs, that of convoking the people and consulting the senate. But side by side with them and in place of them, there were,—for criminal justice and the care of the treasury, the quæstors, whose existence was a check upon their freedom of action even while they were chosen by them, but became a much more prominent one, when they were nominated by the people, which probably took place after the fall of the decemvirs;—for the census and the financial administration, there were the censors, created as occasional magistrates, at the beginning of the fourth century in A.U.C. 311 (B.C. 443), or 319 (B.C. 435);—for the control of order in the city and the markets, there were the two curule ædiles, created in A.U.C. 387, (B.C. 367); —for civil justice, the prætor, also created in A.U.C. 387, and after A.U.C. 512 (B.C. 242), the two prætors, the *praetor urbanus* and the *praetor peregrinus*, who divided amongst themselves, by lot, the judiciary departments; afterwards, also, subsequently to the creation of the provinces, there were other prætors, to whom, for example, were assigned by lot the departments of Sicily, Sardinia, and the two Spains; lastly, after the seventh century, the number of limited jurisdictions was yet again augmented by the *quaestiones perpetuae*, great juries charged with the exclusive repression of certain crimes, and partly presided over by the prætors.

The primitive *imperium* could find its only counterpart in the dictatorship, the extraordinary magistracy which, in the beginning, had no other limitation than its duration (six months at the most) and which was, it is said, a means provided by the constitution for temporarily restoring the monarchy in case of pressing internal or external peril. But precisely at the time when the magistracies were multiplied, the idea of specialisation was applied to the dictatorship; the dictators were created with determinate functions, and there were no more general dictators after the year A.U.C. 538 (B.C. 216). The dictatorship of Sulla and of Cæsar were revolutionary tenures of power which had nothing in common with the ancient dictatorship except the name. On the contrary, Sulla's constitution gave the finishing touch to the system of limited jurisdictions by taking away the military command from the consuls. Henceforward their duty was to remain at Rome during their year of office, like the eight prætors who then existed, and who were charged with civil justice and the six criminal departments, *i.e.,* the six presidencies of *quaestiones perpetuae;* after that the two consuls and the eight prætors, on retiring from office, divided amongst themselves, during the following year, ten governments of provinces, which they held by virtue of a continuation of their powers.

II. **Comitia.** The *comitia* which naturally retained the legislative power and the electoral power, but which almost entirely lost judiciary power in the course of the seventh century, in consequence of the creation of *quaestiones perptuae,* were as in the preceding period: (1) the

comitia curiata, which appear to have been then open
to the plebeians, but had by this time only a formal part
to play (*adrogatio,* promise of allegiance to the new
magistrates, known as *lex curiata de imperio*)—so much
so that the citizens had ceased to trouble themselves to
attend, and were represented by the thirty lictors whose
duty it was to preserve order in the assembly; 2. the
comitia centuriata; 3. the *comitia tributa;* 4. lastly,
side by side with these, the *concilium plebis,* to whom
plenary legislative power thenceforth belonged, who,
that is, thenceforth could make laws obligatory upon
all by virtue of a reform attributed by a most
detailed tradition to three successive laws, and,
at any rate, definitely realized by a *lex Hortensia,* which
comes between A.U.C. 465 (B.C. 289) and A.U.C. 468. In
fine, passing over the *curiae* there were three distinct assemblies with concurrent powers in legislative, electoral
and judiciary matters; and, whilst there was a distribution between the three in the matter of the nomination of
magistrates, and, as long as it existed, in the matter of
criminal justice, legislative power belonged indifferently
to all three of them;—a law could be made indifferently,
either, on the proposition of a tribune, by the *concilium
plebis,* or, on that of a popular magistrate, a consul or a
prætor, by the *comitia tributa* (which must not be confounded with the *concilium plebis*) or by the *comitia centuriata.*

This system appears, at first sight, very singular, and still more so when one observes that any one of these bodies is resorted to indiscriminately, and that constantly projects are referred indifferently to the *concilium plebis* or to the two other assemblies, as may be incidentally the more convenient.

The employment indifferently of the *comitia tributa* and of the *concilium plebis* is explained easily enough by the theory that the distinction between the *plebs* and the entire population, was, in the last centuries, purely historical; and that, the number of the patricians having become very restricted, it came practically to the same thing whether one consulted the tribes without any patricians, or with the few patricians who formed in each only a minute fraction, powerless to displace the majority. But, to explain the fact that one might with equal indifference consult the assembly of the tribes or that of the centuries, it must equally have been the case that, notwithstanding the diversity in the mode of taking the vote, and in the voting unit, there was no practical difference, and that the modern forms of taking the vote had given the essential influence to the same elements in the two assemblies. This idea in fact accords well enough with what we know about them.

The tribes, which at first had been exclusively composed of land owners,—and which, therefore, anciently included only such holders of property,—were opened to all the citizens, whether holders of property or not, at the time of the censorship of the revolutionary nobleman, Appius Claudius, in A.U.C. 442 (B.C. 312). But that in reality did not result in establishing equality of vote; for the censors, to whom belonged the redistribution of the citizens among the tribes, did it in an arbitrary, aristocratic fashion, by including certain categories of citizens in a small number of tribes, where, whatever their number of heads might be, they had only as many voices as there were tribes; whilst the other tribes, containing only rich men or rural proprietors absent from Rome at voting time, formed a crushing majority, notwithstanding their small number of electors. This method had been temporarily employed after the Social war, to secure the majority to the old citizens as against the naturalized Italians. It had by that time been used for a long period, and in a much more drastic manner, against citizens who were not owners of property, who had, since A.U.C. 450 (B.C. 304), been all placed in the four urban tribes, as contrasted with which there were twenty-seven rural tribes at the time of their admission to the vote, and later on thirty-one.

A corresponding system was in reality in practice in the case of the centuries. We have seen that, at the beginning, the number of the centuries of rich men (that is to say, at that time, of persons possessing a certain quantity of land) probably corresponded to their proportion in the total population. This almost necessarily follows when one remembers that the centuries were, at that period, a military unit even more than an electoral

unit, and consequently each must have included, to all
intents and purposes, the same number of soldiers. Later,
on the other hand, when they no longer filled a military rôle, and when, moreover, possessions in general had
been substituted for landed property in the settling
of the census, and when, finally, the development of
Roman power had had for its baneful consequence the
concentration of riches in a small number of hands—there
was nothing to hinder the system becoming, as a consequence, an aristocratic system, giving a majority of votes
to the rich, who, though few in number, had many centuries, while giving a very small number of votes to the
poor, who, though very numerous, were crowded into some
few centuries.   And there are traces that this did happen.   But that did not create any essential difference in
principle between the centuries and the tribes.   Over
and above that, the centuries were reorganized between
A.U.C. 513 (B.C. 241) and A.U.C. 536 (B.C. 218) by a
reform, information concerning which is so meagre that
nearly all the details are disputed, but which increased
the resemblance still further.   It is certain that it suppressed the right of the cavalry to vote first, which had
become for the aristocracy the means of bringing influence to bear on the voting that followed; it is certain, also,
that while allowing the five classes to continue, and the
distinction between *seniores* and *juniores,* and even while
not changing the sum total of the centuries, it somewhat
diminished the number of the centuries of the first class,

and established between the centuries and the tribes some sort of connection which brought the two methods of voting much more closely into harmony. To all intents and purposes, they corresponded in the result, only with a difference of procedure, which rendered the vote of the centuries more imposing, and that of the tribes more expeditious.

III. **Senate.** The senate theoretically preserved the rôle of consultative bòdy; but in reality, in the later period of the Republic, it was the senate which governed the State. This was the result of changes, even more practical than legal, introduced in respect to its attributes as well as the methods by which it was recruited, .

1. *Method of recruiting.* After the *lex Ovinia* of about A.U.C. 442 (B.C. 312) it was the censors who appointed to the senate, instead of the consuls, and they had even the right of renewing it at each census. This might lead us to suppose that its independence in respect to the magistracy had been diminished. But practically it was, on the contrary, rather the freedom of the magistracy which had been restricted. The censors were, except in case of unworthiness, obliged to place in the senate all those who were called to it by occupation of magistracies constantly becoming more numerous. They had no freedom of choice, except as to the holders of the seats, becoming fewer and fewer, which were not occupied by past magistrates. The senate is thus seen to be, at least indirectly, an elective body, composed of magistrates

previously chosen by the people, and without distinction
between patricians and plebeians, save that two functions of the old patrician senate were probably reserved
to patrician senators only,—namely, the *auctoritas
patrum,* which had become a simple formality, and the
interim occupation of power by way of rotation in case
of vacancy, *i.e.,* the *interregnum.*

2. *Attributes.* Approximately speaking, after the
second Punic war, the senate was the true centre of the
government. As regards internal administration, it
was consulted by the magistrates upon all important measures, high matters of police government, (*actes de haute
police*), the proposal of the laws, etc. As regards financial
matters, it determined the employment of the revenue;
it authorized the public works constructed by the censors, and, in the interval between the censorships, by the
consuls and the prætors; and it authorized the payments
made by the quæstors. In military affairs, it settled the
spheres of operation of the generals, and the money
and troops assigned to them; and it arrogated to itself
by usurpation the right of maintaining them in the
discharge of their duties after the expiration of their
powers, whence arose Sulla's system of the double year
of office of the consuls and the prætors, who were sent for
a second year into the provinces by prolongation of their
functions. In the matter of foreign relations, it was
the senate which conducted negotiations and settled
treaties, and, after the making of peace, sent to the

scene of war commissions chosen from its own body
to supervise the execution of the treaties, and organize
the conquered territories. Lastly, in respect to legislation, it already encroached upon the powers of the
comitia by arrogating to itself the right—which it had
been since Sulla more and more openly recognized as
possessing,—of dispensing with the observance of the
laws on urgent occasions or in individual cases(*b*).

2.—*Legislation and the science of the law.*

In the period between the Twelve Tables and the end
of the Republic, the law-making organs multiplied themselves coincidently with the coming into being of the
science of the law. The sources of law were, not only
custom,—which kept its old character of an independent
source, able both to create new law and to abrogate existing law, to introduce new rules, and extinguish established rules, even those established by positive laws;
not only *leges*, which had never been a more active
source, and of which we now, for the first time, find some
concrete examples preserved word for word; but, after
a certain period, *senatusconsulta*, which could modify

(*b*) See Mommsen, *Dr. publ.*, 7, p. 457 *et seq.;* cf. 6, 1, p. 385.
The proof of the constitutional irregularity of its intervention is
that in the case of urgent measures, they were afterwards ordinarily submitted to the ratification of the people, while as to
individual measures, it was precisely these which had been the
object of the older legislative activity of the *comitia* (wills,
adrogation).

existing law in the degree already indicated (note b.), and of which we likewise possess concrete examples(c); and, also, after a certain period, the edicts of the magistrates. Nevertheless, among these four sources, it is only necessary to speak in detail of the *lex*, and the edicts of the magistrates; with which I shall place only the science of the law, which was not in a proper sense at this period a distinct source of law, but which was a very important factor in its elaboration.

I. **Lex.** The name of *lex* comprehends in the period under consideration, in a broad sense, both *leges* properly so called, voted by the *comitia* upon the proposition of a magistrate elected by the whole people, and *plebiscita*, voted by the *plebs* on the proposition of a tribune(d). In both cases what was resolved upon is designated officially by the name of *lex*, which is followed by the family name of the proposer or proposers of the law, in the nominative feminine, *e.g. lex Hortensia, lex Valeria Horatia.* In general, *leges* bear two names when they are consular laws, being considered, from a legal standpoint, as proposed by the two consuls, by virtue of their mutual relationship, even when in fact they only emanate from one of them. On the other hand, they bear only one name when they are proposed by a dictator, who stands alone;—by a prætor, whose relation to his colleagues is of a less close character;—or by a

(c) See the list and examples, *Textes*, p. 120 *et seq.*
(d) Cf. Gaius, 1, 3. *Inst.*, 1, 2, *De j. nat.*, 4.

tribune whose colleagues are too numerous to give all their names to the law(e).

A certain number of laws of the republic have come down to us in inscriptions. For example, the *lex Acilia repetundarum* of A.U.C. 631 or 632 (B.C. 123 or 122), on the repression of the extortions of magistrates, engraved upon a bronze table, of which some fragments are still extant; the agrarian law of A.U.C. 643 (B.C. 111), engraved upon the reverse side of the tablet whose face bears the *lex Acilia;* the *lex Rubria de Gallia Cisalpina*, regulating, in the matter of jurisdictional powers and procedure, the results of the concession of the rights of citizenship to Cisalpine Gaul, and placed by some in A.U.C. 705 (B.C. 49), by others after A.U.C. 712 (B.C. 42), when Cisalpine Gaul was annexed to Italy, and the fourth table of which was found in the eighteenth century at Veleia near to Piacenza; the Este fragment, discovered at Este in 1880, similarly relating to the regulation of jurisdictional powers, which many believe to be a fragment of the same *lex*, and which, in any case, certainly belongs to the same period;(ee) the *lex Julia*, called *Julia Municipalis* of A.U.C. 709 (B.C. 45), relating both to the ordering of the city of Rome, and to the municipal institutions of cities composed of Roman citizens, the first part of which is lost, but the latter part of which we

(e) See on the denomination of *leges*, Mommsen, *Dr. publ.*, 6, 1, p. 359, n. 1; Karlowa, *R. R. G.*, 1, p. 426; Krueger, *Sources*, p. 24, n. 6.

(ce) On the Este fragment, see Appleton, R. gén., 1900, pp. 193-248.

have on two tables of bronze, often called after the place of their discovery, the tables of Heracleia. Lastly may be mentioned, dating from before the end of this period, two examples of what are designated, more or less properly, by the name of *leges datae*, as opposed to *leges rogatae*,—that is to say, as I understand it, laws promulgated by a magistrate by delegation from the people, as were the constitutive laws of provinces or of colonies(*f*) :—a fragment, discovered in 1894, of a municipal statute given to the town of Tarentum, after it had acquired the right of citizenship, in the second half of the seventh century; and some long fragments, discovered at Osuna in 1870 and 1874, of the statute of the citizencolony Julia Genetiva, led into Spain after the death of Cæsar, on the strength of certain laws made during his life(*g*).

This period is, in like manner, the richest in enactments relating to private law. The *comitia* having principally legislated on political matters, and the historians also principally occupying themselves with political laws, these are neither the most numerous kind, nor the kind most frequently mentioned by ancient writers. Nevertheless one may, even omitting the exclusively political laws, and the laws in reference to justice and criminal procedure, which put the *quaestiones* in the place of the

---

(*f*) See on the definition of *leges datae*, Krueger, *Sources*, p. 20, n. 3, and for another view, Mommsen, *Dr. publ.*, 6, 1, p. 253 *et seq.*

(*g*) All these *leges rogatae* or *datae* will be found reproduced in my *Textes*, p. 24 *et seq.*

judiciary *comitia*, cite a fairly large number which relate either to private law or to civil procedure. We shall
have the opportunity of studying all in detail, but it
will not be useless to give a summary list of the principal ones(*h*).

(*h*) It will be observed that the dates which I indicate, devi-
ate noticeably from those, often much more precise, which are
given in the majority of the old books, and have not yet all of
them disappeared from modern books. These latter dates generally arise from the fact that the old authors, eager for precision,
have in the case of laws of which they find the names without
any other information about their date, searched in the fragments
of the Roman lists of magistrates for the corresponding names,
and then made an arbitrary choice among the personages thus
discovered. This process is extremely open to criticism, because
we do not possess these lists complete. If we know nearly all the
consuls, there are quantities of gaps in our lists in the case of
prætors, and still more in the case of tribunes. Therefore it is
perfectly arbitrary to suppose that when a law is called Furia it
is necessarily the law of one or the other of the two or three
Furii mentioned in the texts, when there may have been numbers
of others who were prætors or only tribunes. Besides, this procedure leads to results all the less trustworthy because the chance
nature of what has come down to us, notably the accidental sur-
vival of the work of Livy, supplies us, save as to the last years
of the Republic, principally with information regarding the concluding period of Livy's manuscripts, which, after a break extend-
ing from A.U.C. 461 (B.C. 293) to A.U.C. 536 (B.C. 218), end
at A.U.C. 587 (B.C. 167). Consequently the choices have been
especially made in the period over which we have him, that is,
the fourth, the fifth, and the sixth centuries of the city, while the
laws whose date is certain are nearly all placed between the middle of the sixth century and that of the seventh century (there are
only two or three before that) ; and therefore, the proper inference
would seem to be that the majority should be assigned to that

In the matter of private law, leaving out of account agrarian laws or laws about luxury, we find private laws to which political considerations have certainly given rise: first, the only certain law of the fourth century, the *lex Canuleia*, a *plebiscitum* of A.U.C. 309 (B.C. 445) authorizing marriage between patricians and plebeians; then another law, certainly of the fifth century, the *lex Paetilia Papiria*, ameliorating the condition of debtors, of A.U.C. 428 (B.C. 326) or 441 (B.C. 313), more probably of A.U.C. 428; the laws concerning suretyship, related to politics, in the case of most of them, by their aim of protecting debtors, and in the case of one, by the distinction between Italy and the provinces—the *leges Appuleia, Publilia, Furia, Cicereia,* which have often been attributed to a very early period, but of which one of the

period. On scientific principles the date of a law, when we have no direct evidence as to it, ought to be determined approximately by establishing extreme limits, by deducing from the essential nature of the prevailing institutions, the moment when it cannot yet have existed, and that when it necessarily must have existed already. It is upon this principle —which I have already laid down elsewhere (*R. int., de l'enseignement,* 1890, p. 623 *et seq;* cf. pp. 621-622), and which I have tried to apply to the *lex Aebutia* (*Z. S. St.,* 14, 1893, pp. 11-54=*N. R. hist.,* 1897, pp. 249-294),—that the different dates here indicated have been determined, each one of which will be justified in its place. The recent works of Karlowa and of Krueger do not contain a chronological table relating to private law. Those given in the older works are more or less impaired by the employment of the arbitrary procedure which I have just called attention to. On the other hand valuable hints will be found in the enumeration necessarily summary given by Pernice, *Gesch. und Quell.,* pp. 127-128.

oldest, the *lex Appuleia* presupposes the existence of the provinces, while the first province, Sicily, was founded in A.U.C. 513 (B.C. 241); then the laws concerning gifts, *inter vivos* and testamentary; the *lex Cincia* of A.U.C. 550 (B.C. 204) concerning gifts; the *leges Furia* and *Voconia* about legacies, of which the latter belongs to A.U.C. 585 (B.C. 169), and of which the former, often arbitrarily placed very far back in the past, is posterior to the *lex Cincia,* and finds its place, therefore, between A.U.C. 550 (B.C. 224) and A.U.C. 585 (B.C. 169); strictly speaking, also, another later law concerning legacies, suggested by fiscal considerations, the *lex Falcidia* of A.U.C. 714 (B.C. 40).

Other *leges* were suggested by considerations of purely private law, namely, the *lex Aquilia,* concerning compensation for damage caused to another, which is often placed, on account of very doubtful Byzantine evidence, at the time of the secession of the *plebs* which gave rise to the *lex Hortensia,* and, therefore, between A.U.C. 465 (B.C. 289) and A.U.C. 468 (B.C. 286), but which, in any case, was known to the jurists of the beginning of the seventh century; the *lex Plaetoria* concerning frauds committed against minors under the age of twenty-five years, mentioned as recent in the *Pseudulus* of Plautus, which was acted in A.U.C. 563 (B.C. 191); and lastly, the *lex Atinia,* concerning the usucapion of stolen property, mentioned as recent by the jurists of the end of the sixth century, and the beginning of the seventh century.

In the matter of civil procedure, we find, first, the *lex Paetilia Papiria* of A.U.C. 428 (B.C. 326), which, while it mitigated the condition of debtors, deprived creditors *ex nexo* of the right of *manus injectio;* then, as having established *manus injectio* with modifications, several of the laws mentioned above, the *leges Furiae* concerning suretyship and legacies; the *lex Publilia;* and then a very important law about *manus injectio,* the *lex Vallia,* which finds its place probably towards the end of the sixth century, and which enacted that, in nearly all cases, the defendant in *manus injectio* might be his own *vindex,* might be answerable himself, running the same risks as the *vindex;* lastly, the system of the *actiones legis* was completed, at a very uncertain date, by the creation of a fifth *actio legis,* the *condictio,* established, as to money claims (*certa pecunia*), by a *lex Silia,* and as to claims for other determinate things (*de aliâ certâ re*), by a *lex Calpurnia.*

The last law concerning procedure which finds its place in this period, is the *lex Aebutia,* a law of capital import, not only for procedure, but for private law, which, by the new powers furnished by it to the magistrate rendered the intervention of the legislature almost useless. It introduced a new system of procedure, the formulary procedure—by leaving, as it would seem, to the parties the right of choosing, under the control of the prætor, between the old procedure and the new procedure—and should be assigned, I think, without a doubt, to the first third of the seventh century, between A.U.C. 605 (B.C. 149) —when and even after which date, the old procedure still existed alone —and A.U.C. 628 (B.C. 126), after which evidences of the new procedure begin to present themselves. The characteristic feature from which it derived its name is the *formula*, a statement of the cause of action rendered by the magistrate on the demand of the parties, which instructed the *judex* as to what he was to do in the event of his finding or not finding in favour of the claim of the plaintiff, and which, in the simplest form, instructed him to condemn, in the first case, and to acquit in the second: *si paret. . . condemna, si non paret, absolve*(i).

(i) This formula contains besides the nomination of the *judex*—*Titius judex esto:*—an *intentio: Si paret Numerium Negidium Aulo Agerio sestertium centum milia dare oportere*, and a *condemnatio: condemna, si non paret absolve*. The still more simple *formulae*, those of the *praejudicia*, only contained the nomination of the *judex*, and an *intentio: Titius judex esto an Numerius Negidius Auli Agerii libertus sit*. Others, for example, those of actions *bonae fidei*, contain besides the nomination of the *judex*, before the *intentio* and the *condemnatio*, a *demonstratio* defining the legal grounds of action precisely: *Titius judex esto. Quod Aulus Agerius Numerio Negidio hominem vendidit: quidquid paret Numerio Negidium Aulo Agerio ex bonâ fide, dare facere oportere; judex Numerium Negidium Aulo Agerio condemna, si non paret absolve*. The *formulae* of actions of partition and of settlement of boundaries were the only ones which contained in addition an *adjudicatio* giving the judge the power of transferring the property between the parties: *Quantum adjudicari oportet, judex adjudicato*. These are, then, the four principal parts of the formula: *demonstratio, intentio, adjudicatio, condemnatio*. Besides them the same *formula* may, according to

II. **Edicts of the magistrates**(*j*). Edicts were communications addressed to the public, which, according to the etymology (*ex dicere*) were at first oral, but which, in the later sense of the word, denoted in addition to that, communications publicly posted up. In this broad acceptation of the word, edicts might issue from anybody whomsoever, even from private individuals, and it is not impossible to cite texts in support of this view. But, without, perhaps, having an absolutely different character, they naturally assumed quite a different import when they emanated from public authorities, who had recourse to them to secure, either as against everybody, or as against certain individuals, the effect of separate notification. And this is the point of view of those who speak of authorities possessing the *jus edicendi,* or who enumerate the edicts which have come down to us(*k*).

circumstances, contain or not contain, certain accessory parts, for example, *praescriptiones,* placed at the head, either in the interest of the plaintiff, or in the interest of the defendant; or *exceptiones,* submitting to the *judex* a second question in the interest of the defendant, or *replicationes,* submitting to him, a third in the interest of the plaintiff, &c. Cf. Gaius, 4, 39-44, 115, 137, and the explanations given in book IV. of the present work.

(*j*) Krueger, *Sources,* p. 40 *et seq.;* Bruns-Lenel, *Gesch. und Quell.,* secs. 27-29. See also in the *Grande Encyclopédie* my two articles *Droit prétorien* and *Edits des magistrats,* and in book IV. of my *Manuel,* the chapter in the formulary procedure.

(*k*) See on the *jus edicendi,* Mommsen, *Dr. publ.,* 1, p. 230 *et seq.* Examples of the principal edicts which have come down to us, *Textes,* p. 159 *et seq.*

But the edicts thus understood did not form a source of law. It was by way of development of one of their varieties (the edicts issued upon entry into office), that the edicts of certain magistrates,—those, namely, who had charge of the civil administration of justice,—became, subsequently to a definite piece of legislation (the passing of the *lex Aebutia*) a very abundant source of law, which placed the *jus praetorium* side by side with the *jus civile*.

Roman magistrates of a certain rank —consuls, censors, prætors, governors of provinces, for example —were accustomed to publish, upon their entry into office, a kind of manifesto in which they introduced themselves to those under their authority by informing them of their credentials and their projects. We have in them at first only a species of rather vague proclamations, of political professions of faith published after their election, wherein there was often more prominence given to family connections or to past acts of a new magistrate, than to his intended acts; and which, in any case, did not bind him any more than political professions of faith do nowadays. But whilst these edicts upon entry into office always retained the same character in the case of the consuls and censors, those of the judiciary magistrates —the urban and peregrin prætors, and curule ædiles at Rome, and governors and their accompanying quæstors, the latter of whom discharged the functions of curule ædiles, in the provinces—assumed, after the *lex Aebutia,* quite a different rôle, corresponding to the increase of the powers of the magistrates(*l*).

Up to that time, the judiciary magistrates, having little more to do than assist, in the manner prescribed by the law, in the carrying through of the *legis actio,* had not been able to promise in their edicts judiciary reforms which were beyond their powers. The most the prætors had then been able to promise,—as is commonly admitted, principally on the strength of theoretical considerations, —was to supply deficiencies of the law, in virtue of their general police powers, by resorting to two or three processes, which we shall often meet again,—the *missiones in possessionem,* by which, to bring pressure to bear upon the will of a man (for example, to make him come out of a place where he was hiding himself) another man was permitted to install himself in possession of some property of his,—the prætorian stipulations, where the magistrate compelled a man to enter, by verbal contract, into an engagement necessary for the security of a third person,—the interdicts or orders which he imposed upon a person, on the demand of an interested party, by for-

(*l*) Gaius, 1, 6 (cf. Justinian, *Inst.,* 1, 2, *De j. nat.,* 7): *Amplissimum jus est in edictis duorum praetorum urbani et peregrini, quorum in provinciis juris dictionem praesides carum habent; item in edictis aedilium curulium, quorum juris dictionem in provinciis populi Romani quaestores habent, 4, 11: Tunc (in the time of the actiones legis) edicta praetorum quibus complures actiones introductae sunt in usu non erant.*

bidding their contravention. But they could neither promise to give actions which the law did not give, nor to refuse those which it did give. And this was true, as I think, not only in the case of the urban prætor, but also of the governors, the ædiles, and the *praetor peregrinus* at any rate in respect to Roman citizens, who could not be deprived of actions which the law gave them, nor be sued in actions which the law did not give against them.

On the other hand, after the *lex Aebutia*, the magistrates acquired new powers. This law placed the *formula* by the side of the *legis actio*, by permitting parties to choose between the two under the supervision of the magistrate. It consequently imposed upon the magistrate the duty of transposing into *formulae*, as occasion arose, the sacramental words previously spoken by the pleaders in order to join in each of the known forms of legal process; and by that very fact, it gave him quite a new authority over legal process, both over the old *legis actio*, which could no longer be brought without his consent, and also over the *formula*, which derived its existence from him. It opened to him, probably in a fashion rather unconscious than deliberate, the path of legislative reforms, by permitting him to stifle pretensions founded on the law, when he refused the *legis actio* without delivering any correlative *formula*(m), and by per-

(m) This is the *denegatio legis actionis*, which is often represented as dating back to the times of the *actiones legis*, but the known examples of which are all later than the *lex Aebutia*, and which, in my view, before that would have constituted a forfeiture on the part of the magistrate (*N. R. hist.*, 1897, p. 258, n. 1; p. 271, n. 3).

mitting him, conversely, to sanction pretensions without a legal basis, when he delivered *formulae* which corresponded only imperfectly, or did not correspond at all, to existing laws. And it is precisely the exercise of this power on the part of the magistrate, particularly on the part of the prætor, which gave a new importance to his edict upon the entry into office,—the manifesto in which he set forth technically and precisely the programme of his judicial administration.

In less than a century, this programme, called *edictum perpetuum*,—that is to say, a standing edict, issued for the whole year of office, by way of contrast to *edicta repentina*, occasioned by some accidental circumstances,—had developed into a long ordinance, posted up near the magistrate's tribunal, upon boards of white wood (*album*). The magistrate, on the one hand, set forth in it concrete forms of pleas which might be demanded of him (*formulae*) (*n*); and, on the other hand, indicated in it under what conditions he would grant them or refuse them (*edicta* in the narrow sense) (*o*), by drawing up formulas both for actions given by the law (*actiones civiles*) and for those given by himself, but not pledging himself in his edicts excepting as to the new remedies

(*n*) Examples, Gaius, 4, 37; *Lex Rubria*, 20, 1.

(*o*) Thus *judicium dabo, actionem non dabo, possessionem dabo, promitti jubebo, in integrum restituam, &c.* See the edicts preserved, *Textes*, p. 131 *et seq.*

given by himself, which alone needed his promise(*p*), and which comprised thenceforth not only the *missiones in possessionem*, the prætorian stipulations, and the interdicts, but a number of other instruments of procedure, prætorian actions, exceptions, prescriptions, and *restitutiones in integrum*. He announced, for example, that, whilst, according to the *jus civile*, a contract obtained by fraud was nevertheless valid, he would give to the victim of the fraud an *exceptio* whereby to escape from carrying out such an engagement,—that is to say, he would insert in the *formula* of the action a clause telling the *judex* to pass judgment only *si in eâ re nihil dolo malo Auli Agerii* (the conventional name of the plaintiff) *factum sit neque fiat*, (the *exceptio doli mali*) ;—that, whilst the victim of a theft could not under the *jus civile* claim compensation due from the thief, unless they were both of them citizens, he would none the less give an action, when the other conditions were present, by directing the *judex* to determine the case as though the parties had the qualification of citizens, by supposing by way of fiction the existence of this qualification, (the prætorian *actio fictitia*) ;—that, whilst the *jus civile* did not recognize the

(*p*) This difference between the civil actions, of which the *praetor* merely gave the *formula*, and the praetorian actions, which he expressly promised before giving the *formula* of them, has been brought out with especial clearness by Wlassak, *Edict und Klageform*, 1882, and has been, in my opinion, very strongly confirmed despite certain difficulties of detail by the researches of Lenel, in regard to the edict of Julianus (p. 115, n. l.).

creation of a hypothec, he would give to the creditor to whom a thing had been appropriated as security by agreement, an action by which to claim its possession from anyone who detained it (the prætorian *actio in factum*);—that, whilst the *jus civile* held the debts of one who had given himself in arrogation to be extinguished by a civil death, (a *capitis deminutio*,) he would, for the benefit of creditors, replace things in the position in which they would have been if there had never been a *capitis deminutio* (the *restitutio in integrum*).

These different provisions, introduced successively by different prætors, and most of them preserving in their name the remembrance of their authors(*q*), constituted, as contrasted with the *jus civile*, the *jus praetorium*—or, more broadly, as including the edicts of all the judicial magistrates, the *jus honorarium*(*r*),—established, said the Romans, to aid, supplement, or correct, the *jus civile*(*s*): and its judicial foundation in my opinion lies,—not, as was said, more especially in former days, in a happy usurpation by the prætor and by similar magistrates, nor, as is still said, in a delegation

(*q*) *Formulae Rutiliana, Octaviana, Fabiana, Actiones Pauliana, Publiciana, Judicium Cascellianum, Edictum Carbonianum, Interdictum Salvianum,* for example.

(*r*) From *honos* a magistracy, *Inst.,* 1, 2, *De j. nat.,* 7. Cf. nevertheless Krueger, *Sources,* p. 49, n. 1.

(*s*) Papinian, *D.,* 1, 1, *De j. et j.,* 7, 1: *Jus praetorium est, quod praetores induxerunt adjuvandi vel supplendi vel corrigendi juris civilis gratia propter utilitatem publicam.* Cf. Marcianus, *D.,* h. t., 8.

for their benefit of the legislative power, which never took place, nor even in the exercise by them of the general powers of the magistrates,—but in the exercise by them of the special power of organizing legal procedure, which the *lex Aebutia* conferred upon them.

The rules of the prætorian law were distinguished externally, in the *album*, from those of the *jus civile*, by the material and tangible fact of the existence of the edicts establishing them, which, more than anything else, must have emphasized the contrast. Beyond that, they differed from them by three apparent points of inferiority: 1. Whilst a *lex* was perpetual, an edict could only be invoked during the year of office of the magistrate who had promulgated it; and, moreover, even during that year it was not strictly obligatory upon its author, until the *lex Cornelia* of A.U.C. 687 (B.C. 67), which forbade magistrates departing from the engagements entered into by them in their edicts in respect to those subject to their jurisdiction(*t*). 2. Unlike a *lex*, which extended throughout all the territory of the Empire, an edict (the legislative function of which was not older than the system of limited powers) was only appli-

---

(*t*) Asconius, *in Ciceronem, Pro Cornel.* (ed. Kiessling and Schoell, 1875, p. 52): *Aliam deinde legem Cornelius* (tr. pl. 687) *etsi nemo repugnare ausus est, multis tamen invitis tulit: ut praetores ex edictis suis perpetuis jus dicerent: quae res cunctam gratiam ambitiosis praetoribus, qui varie jus dicere assueverant sustulit.* Previously, the praetor, *qui aliter ut edixerat decernit,* could perhaps be stopped by the *intercessio* of his colleague. See Cicero, *In Verr.,* 2, 1, 46, 119, and Mommsen, *Dr. publ.,* 1, p. 237.

cable within the jurisdiction of the magistrate who had issued it. 3. Lastly, unlike *leges*, edicts could not directly abrogate a rule of law or create a new one; they could only arrive practically at the same result, neutralise practically the law where it was defective. He who was fraudulently brought under a legal obligation was a debtor *jure civili*; the prætor did not say that he should no longer be so, he only said: *Exceptionem dabo.* *Capitis deminutio* extinguished debts; the prætor did not say that it should not extinguish them, but only said: *In integrum restituam.* In the same way, when he called an heir, whom statutory law did not call, he did not say: *Heres esto, familiam habeto;* he said: *Bonorum possessionem dabo.* He could neither make nor unmake *jus civile.* He could only permit disregard of the *lex* which made or unmade it.

But these inferiorities are only apparent. In respect to the one last mentioned, the edict by its oblique methods of procedure arrived as surely at its goal as the *lex* by its direct dispositions, and, in case of conflict, it was the former which prevailed. If in law the edict only applied within the circle of its author's jurisdiction, in fact the provisions of the edicts of the capital were reproduced in each province by magistrates placed at the head of the administration of justice, with only such differences as were rendered advantageous by local conditions(*u*).

(*u*) Cicero relates, *Ad. Att.*, 6, 1, 15, that in Cilicia, after having specified in his edict certain points relating to local law or demanding special regulating, he referred for the rest to the urban edicts. Cf. *Ad Fam.*, 3, 8, 4.

Lastly, if in law the edict only lasted one year,—a cir-
cumstance, however, which had the advantage of permitting unfortunate provisions to drop out—the edict of a
magistrate leaving office was immediately replaced by
that of the entering magistrate, in which re-appeared
provisions, sanctified by long usage from the edicts of
former magistrates. This *pars translaticia*, transmitted
from magistrate to magistrate, necessarily always formed
the greater part of the whole edict as contrasted with the
pars nova, constituted by the creations of the actual mag-
istrate(*v*). Indeed, the edict probably already contained,
by the end of the Republic, the great majority of the
rules which were to find a place in its definitive codifi-
cation(*w*).

(*v*) Cicero, *In Verr.*, 2, 1, 44, 114: *Hoo edictum vetus trans-
laticiumque est.* 15, 115: *In re vetere edictum novum*, 48, 117:
Hoo ediotum translaticium esse. Ad Att., 5, 21, 11: *Cum ego in
edicto translaticio . . haberem.* The predominance of the
pars translaticia over the *pars nova* resulted also from the appearance of the commentaries: the first is that in twelve books of Scr.
Sulpicius, consul in A.U.C. 703, died in A.U.C. 711 (B.C. 43).

(*w*) Light is still needed on two points:—1. In what
chronological order the different dispositions of the edict were
introduced. This is a question upon which there are many
scattered writings, but there is not as yet any general work
excepting a very short, though interesting study, by Dernburg,
Festagabe für Heffter, 1873, p. 93 *et seq.* 2. What was the
material arrangement of the edict; and whether, for, example, the
edicts in a strict sense and the formulas of actions were not
separated into two distinct tables, instead of being joined together, as later, in a single table, giving the formulas for each
form of plea, and, where there were any, the edicts relating to
them. See Wlassak, *Edict und Klogeform*, 1882; Girard, *N. R.
hist.*, 1904, pp. 158-103.

III. The Science of the law in the Republican Period(x).

At Rome, as elsewhere, the law when once expressed in its abstract form by legislative enactment, required interpretation by competent men (*jurisprudentes*), who should apply it to concrete cases. The interpretation of the law, the science of the law—*juris prudentia, jus civile* in the strict sense(y)—during the period which

(x) Krueger, *Sources*, §§ 4, 7-9; Bruns-Lenel, *Gesch. und Quell.*, §§ 17, 18, 30-32. Cf. P. Joers, *Römische Rechtswissenschaft zur Zeit der Republik*, 1 (up to the Catos), 1888. Bremer, *Jurisprudentia antehadriana*, 1 (period of the Republic), 1896.

(y) Ehrlich, *Beiträge zur Theorie der Rechtsquellen*, L. 1902, has brought out very well this the most restricted and probably the oldest sense of the term *jus civile*, which is strikingly described by the contemporary of Hadrian, Pomponius, *D.*, 1, 2, *De o. j.*, 2, 12: *Est proprium jus civile quod sine scripto in solâ prudentium interpretatione consistet*, and in which sense the texts appear to contrast directly the *jus civile* with the positive law resulting, for example, from the vote of the *comitia* (see Cicero, *De Oratore*, 34, 120: *Quid est enim turpius quam legitimarum et civilium controversiarum patrocinia suscipere cum sis legum et civilis juris ignarus?*). And we may admit with him that it is by way of opposition to the pretorian law that the expression afterwards came to assume a wider meaning, embracing the rules resulting from the *leges*, the *senatusconsulta*, and the imperial constitutions. But Ehrlich seems to me to go too far when he maintains that this restricted meaning was the only one known up to the time of the Severan Emperors. Not only is he obliged to recognize that the word is employed in earlier times in an acceptation large enough to include the legislative arrangements relative to the matter of successions, or proceeding from the Twelve Tables; and not only does he fail to do away with the force of a text of Papinian, *D.*, 1, 1, *De j. et j.*, 7, 1, who defines the word in the broad sense, embracing at the same time the *leges*,

extends from the formulation of the Twelve Tables to the end of the Republic, passed through three successive phases: an esoteric phase, when the law was kept a secret; a phase of popularisation, during which the knowledge of it was spread abroad in a practical manner, without care for theoretical order of exposition; and a phase of systematisation, when appeared the first works on legal doctrine written on a general plan.

The first phase, which lasted until the middle of the fifth century, was the phase of secrecy, according to very

the *senatusconsulta*, the imperial constitution, and the decisions of the jurisconsults; but beyond all that, the text of Pomponius, *D.*, 1, 2, *De o. j.*, 2, which indicates the restricted meaning in paragraph 12, clearly seems to oppose to it the broad sense in paragraph 5, where he says that the *disputatio fori* and the law made by the *prudentes propriâ parte (appellatione?) aliquâ non appellatur ut ceterae partes juris suis nominibus designantur.* . . . *sed communi nomine appellatur jus civile,* that is to say,—translated in the most natural way,—while the other sources of the *jus civile* have, besides this common general name, each one an individual name, the law, made by the jurisconsults, is only designated by the general name; and it is not impossible that Cicero had previously opposed the *jus civile* to the pretorian law in the same sense (*Pro Coecinâ*, 12, 34: *nam quid ages mecum ex jure civili ac praetorio non habes*). This harmonizes perfectly with the explanation of the change suggested by Ehrlich, if one remembers that the circumstances which gave the word the new broad meaning in this system of law, had existed not only since the codification of the Edict, as it was in the time of Pomponius, but ever since it commenced to assume a certain importance, as it had done as far back as the time of Cicero. Cf. Kipp, *Geschichte der Quellen,* p. 94, n. 33; Lambert, *Mélanges Appleton,* 1903, p. 54, n. 1; Erman, *Z. S. St.* 24, 1903, pp. 421-440; and the reply of Ehrlich to Erman, *Zeitschrift de Grünhut,* 1904, pp. 331-364.

precise Roman tradition. The science of the law was then, at any rate, as a matter of fact, and very generally the monopoly of the pontiffs(z). By reason of the relations between private law and religion, by reason of the influence of the calendar upon justice, by reason also, perhaps, of the primitive religious character of the *sacramentum*, they certainly had, in spite of manifold obscurities, a serious influence upon the practice of law; and one can readily believe that they tried to make out of the knowledge of this practice a sort of secret science, a sort of private monopoly of their order.

Undoubtedly the writers of later times exaggerate when they say that all the law was kept a secret by the pontiffs(a). It was public in its abstract form, seeing that the Twelve Tables were posted up at the *comitium*. It was public in its concrete application, seeing that justice was administered publicly in the same place. But behind this exaggeration there is an element of truth. The proper mode of setting the law in operation was certainly unknown to the people. A man of the Roman people, it has been said, would have been as much at a loss how to apply the Twelve Tables to a given situation, as a man of the people of to-day would be in the use of a table of

(z) Pomponius,*D.*, 1, 2, *De o. j.*, 2, 6: *Harum* (the Twelve Tables) *et interpretandi scientia et actiones apud collegium pontificum erant.*

(a) Livy, 9, 46, 5: *Jus civile reconditum in penetralibus pontificum.* Cf. Cicero, *De Orat.*, 1, 41, 186.

logarithms. Accordingly, just as the Romans, in later times, went to consult lay jurisconsults in order to know the forms according to which to transact legal business, and to get their cases tried, so in ancient times they sought out the pontiffs for such purposes(*b*). Unlike later legal counsel, those of that time left no names. Their work was anonymous as well as collective,—and precisely because collective. But that did not make it any the less important.

From the time of the Twelve Tables (as doubtless already before that) down to the middle of the fifth century, the pontiffs practically had the science of the law centred in themselves. And, as always happens with legal doctrine and practice, they created by way of interpretation, under the stress of daily needs, much new law,—all the new law which was made in this period, in which we have no trace of *leges* relating to private law, and in which the activity of the prætor (which is a serious factor only after the date of the *lex Aebutia*) had not begun. Thus it was that they probably brought into existence at that time all those legal methods, prompted by expediency, and derived from the employment of legal machinery for an object different to its normal object, which are very numerous in ancient Roman law, and which comprise, for example, enfranchisement, *in jure cessio*, eman-

(*b*) It is doubtless to these consultations that the very obscure statement of Pomponius relates, *D.*, 1, 2, *De o. j.*, 2, 6, about the college of pontiffs *ex quibus constituebatur quis quoquo anno praeesset privatis.*

cipation, adoption, the will *per aes et libram*, and many other juristic acts.

This first phase ended and the second commenced in the middle of the fifth century by a very well known event, the divulging of the *formulae* by Cn. Flavius, secretary of the celebrated Appius Claudius Cæcus(*c*), and son of one of his freedmen. He published, in a collection called the *jus Flavianum*, the *formulae* of the *legis actiones*, which, it is said, he stole from his patron, but which, judging from the tendencies of the patron, the latter must rather have published through him as his intermediary. As a reward, he was appointed curule ædile for A.U.C. 450 (B.C. 304), which implies that the publication took place a little before A.U.C. 450. Besides that, he is represented as having posted up the calendar in such a way as to render it unnecessary to resort to the pontiffs to know the juridical days, apparently a second distinct action of his, performed by him perhaps in the capacity of curule ædile in A.U.C. 450. One may associate with Flavius' conduct, that of the first plebeian *pontifex maximus*, T. Coruncanius, consul in A.U.C. 474 (B.C. 280), who was the first *publice profiteri*(*d*),— which probably means to conduct his consultations in public, before listeners who could take notes of them, and could thus acquire by degrees legal instruction of a

(*c*) Pomponius, *D.*, 1, 2, *De o. j.*, 2, 7; Livy, 9, 46, 5; Cicero, *Ad Att.*, 6, 1, 8; *Pro Mur.*, 11, 25; Pliny, *H. N.*, 33, 1, 17.

(*d*) Pomponius, *D.*, 1, 2, *De o. j.*, 2, 35, 38.

general character, following a method which was for long the only serious mode of instruction in the law (e).

From that time the science of the law became secularised, and those who wanted to attract popular favour, and thereby reach the magistracies, could set themselves to give legal advice to all comers,—advice especially indispensable because of the formal character of the law and of the procedure, and especially in demand because of its gratuitous character, which doubtless led to the jurisconsults being more willingly sought after than modern lawyers. We find examples of their social position in anecdotes such as that of Scipio Nasica, to whom the senate voted a house on the *Via Sacra* that he might be more conveniently at the disposal of those who desired consultations with him; or that of C. Figulus, who sought to make use of his popularity as a counsel to procure his appointment as consul (f).

Consultation (*respondere*),—along with which was still placed the drawing up of legal documents (*cavere*), and also sometimes the conduct of legal process (*agere*) (g),—

(e) See upon this form of instruction Cicero, *Orat.*, 42, 143. *Brut.*, 89, 306: (Q. Mucius Scaevola) *nemini se ad docendum dabat, tamen consultantibus respondendo studiosos audiendi docebat.*

(f) Pomponius, *D.*, 1, 2, *De o. j.*, 2, 37; Val. Max., 9, 3, 2. Cf. Cicero, *De Off.*, 2, 19, 65.

(g) Cicero, *De Orat.*, 1, 48, 212. Elsewhere, for example, *De Off.*, 2, 19, 65, he speaks only of consulting and of *cavere*. Cf. *Pro Murenâ*, 9, 19 (regarding Servius Sulpicius): *Urbana militia respondendi scribendi cavendi.*

was probably the principal occupation of the greater part of the jurisconsults of this epoch, and of the following century, amongst whom I will only mention Sextus Aelius Paetus Catus, consul in A.U.C. 556 (B.C. 198); M. Porcius Cato, the censor in A.U.C. 520-605 (B.C. 234-149); his son M. Porcius Cato Licinianus, who died in A.U.C. 602 (B.C. 152); then three men who are represented to us as having founded the *jus civile*(h) :— M. Manilius, consul in A.U.C. 605 (B.C. 149), P. Mucius Scaevola, consul in A.U.C. 621 (B.C. 133), and M. Junius Brutus, nearly their contemporary; lastly, P. Rutilius Rufus, consul in A.U.C. 649 (B.C. 105), prætor later in A.U.C. 636 (B.C. 118), the first jurisconsult whose name is associated with the history of the edict as it was developed after the *lex Aebutia*. These jurisconsults published certain works, Sextus Aelius publishing the *Tripertita* (which set forth, either in successive order or under the topic of each institution, the Twelve Tables, the *interpretatio*, and the *legis actiones*) and a *Jus Aelianum*, as to which it is a question whether we ought to see in it a distinct work, or the third part of the *Tripertita*, or only an invention of recent writers suggested by its harmony with the *Jus Flavianum*; M. Manilius, a collection of *formulae*; P. Mucius Scævola, a work in ten books; lastly, Brutus, three books *De jure civili*, written a little awkwardly in imitation of the Greek philosophers, under the form of conversations with his son. But, with the

(h) Pomponius, *D.*, 1, 2, *De o. j.*, 2, 39.

exception perhaps of that of Brutus, these writings were still doubtless of a purely practical character, and were simple collections of forms and precedents, compiled without any systematic design(*i*).

The third period begins with the son of P. Mucius Scaevola, Q. Mucius Scaevola, governor of Asia, consul in A.U.C. 659 (B.C. 95), slain in A.U.C. 672 (B.C. 82) by the partisans of Marius. He composed a *Jus Civile* in eighteen books, which was, to all appearance, the first methodical exposition of the *jus civile*, the plan of which afterwards inspired that of the *Jus Civile* of Sabinus. and which was frequently cited and commented on by the authors of the time of the Empire(*j*).

It will be sufficient for us to name among the later jurisconsults who continued to walk in the same paths:—Aquilius Gallus, prætor in A.U.C. 688 (B.C. 66); Servius Sulpicius, consul in A.U.C. 703 (B.C. 51), who died in A.U.C. 711 (B.C. 43), author in particular of the first commentary on the edict (two books *ad edictum*). who had for his pupils nearly all the jurisconsults of the end of the Republic, notably Alfenus Varus, supple-

(*i*) We owe also, without doubt, to the activity of the authors of this period, frequently designated 'the *veteres*' by the jurisconsults of the time of the Empire, a large part of the general rules formulated in maxims which these last quote to us and some of which have retained the name of their inventor (*regula Catoniana, praesumptio Muciana*, for example). See concerning these *regulae*, Bruns-Lenel, *Gesch. und Quell.*, p. 135.

(*j*) See on the plan of this work, Lenel, *Das Sabinussystem*, 1892, p. 10, *et seq.*

7—ROM. LAW.

mentary consul in A.U.C. 715 (B.C. 39), and Aulus Ofilius, an intimate of Cæsar's, who also wrote a commentary on the edict; lastly Cascellius, who was probably prætor after the death of Cæsar; C. Trebatius Testa, whose life extended for long years under the reign of Augustus; and Q. Aelius Tubero, who gave up the bar for the science of law, after having been defeated by Cicero in the matter of the accusation framed by him against Q. Ligarius(k).

(k) The extant citations, direct or indirect, from the juridical writings of the different jurisconsults, which, especially from the time of Q. Mucius Scaevola, are sufficiently abundant to permit of serious research, are collected together under the name of each in Lenel, *Palingenesia juris civilis.* Huschke, pp. 1-18, pp. 84-109, and Bremer, 1, give furthermore a certain number of fragments relating to public and religious law excluded by the plan of Lenel's work. The student may refer for a more detailed history of their lives and labours to the works already mentioned of Krueger, Bruns-Lenel, and Bremer. For a complete enumeration of the materials for juridical study left by Republican times, there remains to be mentioned,—along with the fragments of laws, *senatusconsulta,* edicts of magistrates and writings of jurisconsults, which have been preserved,—if not concrete legal documents, which for this period are almost entirely wanting (see, as the sole exception, the building contract of Pizzuoli of A.U.C. 649 (B.C. 105), *Textes,* p. 815, at any rate the material furnished by general literature. Amongst them the history of Polybius, who died in A.U.C. 627 (B.C. 127), which runs from the first Punic war to the fall of Carthage and Corinth, is an excellent historical source, but richer for public law than for private law. The treatise on rural economy (*de re rusticâ*) of Cato contains, especially at c. 144-145, some precedents which are very instructive for the history of the origins of letting and of partnership (Bruns, *Fontes,* 2, pp. 49-53; cf. Bekker, Z. R. G., 3, 1864, pp. 416-445). There is also much precious information in the works of Varro, who died in A.U.C. 727 (B.C. 27): for example in the precedents of sales of slaves and of animals in his treatise *de re rusticâ* (passages relating to law are in Bruns, *Fontes*, pp. 53-59). Lastly, the two sources which are most prolific, though different, are: 1. The plays of Plautus, who died in A.U.C. 570 (B.C. 184), and whose extant productions, which find their place between A.U.C. 549 (B.C. 205) and A.U.C. 570 (B.C. 184) are Roman adaptations of Greek pieces, where the plot remains Greek, but where there are, especially in matters of detail, many additions, drawn from Roman juridical sources. There is an abstract of the juridical passages in Costa, *Diritto privato Romano nelle comedie di Plauto*, 1890; cf. *N. R. hist.*, 1893, pp. 795-797: add for the plays of Terence, which are still more Greek, and for some other extracts, Bekker, *Z. S. St.*, 13, 1892, pp. 53-118. 2. The works of Cicero, born in January A.U.C. 648 (B.C. 106), died in December A.U.C. 711 (B.C. 43), whose speeches in civil and criminal matters, and also his correspondence and all his productions, are a mine of information on public and private law, worked for centuries and almost inexhaustible. The book of Caqueray, *Explication des passages de droit privé dans les œuvres de Cicéron*, 1857, is antiquated and incomplete; but there is no general collection more recent. Amongst the innumerable separate dissertations I shall only mention the commentaries, themselves a little old now, upon some of the civil forensic speeches by Keller, *Semestria ad Ciceronem*, 1842-1851, and Bethmann-Hollweg, *Civilprozess*, 2, 1865, pp. 784-841.

CHAPTER III.—THE EMPIRE.

SECTION I.—THE PRINCIPATE.

If we date its commencement from A.U.C. 727 (B.C. 27), and its termination at the accession of Diocletian, in the year A.D. 284, the principate founded by Augustus occupies in Roman history a period of more than 300 years. It is on the law of this period that we have most documents, and this is also the period when the most celebrated jurisconsults flourished, and, therefore, the one in which the history of the law and of its interpreters demands most expansive treatment. The political constitution, on the other hand, may be sketched in a few words.

1.—*Organisation of the State*(a).

Augustus said, in his political testament, speaking of the abdication, in A.U.C. 727 (B.C. 27), of his extra-

(a) It would serve no purpose to incumber with bibliographical citations this brief reference to a condition of things the treatment of which has filled volumes. The most complete and juridical work on the principate is that which composes volume 5 . of Mommsen's *Droit public*. Paragraphs 33 to 38 of Bruns-Lenel may also be consulted with profit.

ordinary powers in order to put the new constitution into operation, that he was then taking the State out of his own hands and placing it under the authority of the senate and of the people(*b*). And there are many who, without exaggerating to this extent, yet, on the strength of the division of powers made between the prince and the senate, designate the régime established by Augustus by the name of "diarchy," *i.e.*, government by the emperor and the senate, in contrast with government by an individual, such as the monarchy of Diocletian and Constantine. The contrast made between the two régimes is a true one. The principate was not as yet the open despotism of Byzantine law. It had the hybrid character of equivocal institutions designed to realise in outward form transitions already accomplished in fact. But, nevertheless, in fact, and even in law, the emperor had already in this period a preponderance, which was no doubt accentuated first under Hadrian, and then under the Severan emperors, but which existed potentially from the time of Augustus, as the necessary result of the form which he gave to the three elements of the prior constitution.

1. *Comitia.*—The judiciary power of the *comitia* which, by reason of the development of the procedure of the *quaestiones*, scarcely continued to exist in the last period of the Republic, vanished completely from the time of Augustus. As to their electoral power, it survived, in-

(*b*) *Mon. Ancyr.*, 6, 12: *Rem publicam ex meâ potestate in senatus populique Romani arbitrium transtuli.*

deed, under Augustus, but it was taken away from them and transferred to the senate as early as the first year of Tiberius, B.C. 14(c). Their legislative power itself did not survive very long. They still exercised it somewhat actively under Augustus, and during the first half of the reign of Tiberius; but after that they were only able to do so occasionally. We meet only a few comitial laws under Claudius, and a single and final one under Nerva. The electoral power and the legislative power of the *comitia* had practically disappeared before the end of the reign of Tiberius, with the sole exception of the vote by acclamation by means of which the *comitia* confirmed, on the accession of a new emperor, the *senatusconsultum* proposing to bestow upon him the tribunitial and certain other powers.

2. *Senate.*—The senate inherited the power of the *comitia* over elections, and also up to a certain point, as we shall see, their legislative power. It shared with the emperor the judiciary power. It had the supreme administration of the provinces called senatorial, or popular, provinces, by contrast to the imperial provinces. It also had the revenues which issued from these provinces, and which fell into the *acrarium*, or public treasury, by contrast to the receipts which fell into the new treasury of the prince, *fiscus principis*. And it is principally in view of this division of judiciary, administrative, and financial

(o) Tacitus, Ann., 1, 15: *Tum primum e campo comitia ad patres translata sunt.*

powers, that people have qualified the system by the name of "diarchy." But of the two authorities the stronger was that of the emperors, who had become not only the first of the magistrates, but magistrates stronger than the *comitia* and the senate.

3. *Magistracies.*—The first magistrate was the sovereign, the emperor, upon whose head were concentrated afresh all the powers which the Republic had divided among the different magistrates. But we must not see in that a reversion to the concentration of powers which existed in other days for the benefit of the kings and the first consuls. The imperial authority had for its essential basis two powers unknown to the epoch of the kings:— the proconsular *imperium,* the outcome of the system of prorogation of office, and the tribunitial power, the outcome of the plebeian institutions. The *princeps* received the proconsular *imperium* from the senate or from the army; then the people transferred to him, in the law of which I have just spoken—that law which the texts of the period of decadence, and they alone, speak of as the *lex regia*—the tribunitial power, and ·a certain number of other special jurisdictions, the list of which was extended as time went on. These were the two necessary and sufficient bases of his predominance. He was inviolable by virtue of his tribunitial power, which, unlike that of the tribunes, was unlimited in time and space. He was also for that reason superior to all the magistrates. He possessed, by virtue of his proconsular *imperium,* which was

in like manner extended to the whole empire, the exclusive command of all the troops, and the right of appointing to all ranks. He had the exclusive right of concluding treaties, and of making peace or war. And that, without taking into account anything else, would have sufficed to place him above the senate, even if the division of provinces, of judiciary authority, and of financial powers, had been observed literally. But, indeed, it never was so: he had from the first a right of preference, in case of conflict, in judiciary matters; he soon intervened, by virtue of his stronger proconsular *imperium*, in the administration of the senatorial provinces; and in financial matters, he not only kept constantly increasing the ambit of the receipts of the *fiscus* at the expense of that of the receipts of the *aerarium*, but indeed he succeeded, as early as the first century and the days of Nero, in becoming as completely master of the public treasury, at the head of which he placed prefects of his own choice, as he was of his private treasury.

It is true, the magistrates of the Republic,—consuls, prætors, tribunes, ædiles, quæstors,—still continued to be annually chosen, and the consuls and prætors continued to go as governors, after the expiration of their powers, into the senatorial provinces. But, not to mention the influence which the emperor had upon their election, these magistrates had become exclusively civil and subordinate authorities, deprived of all military powers, and dominated in everything by himself and his agents.

As to military powers, the governors of the provinces themselves had none, for there were no troops in the senatorial provinces, except at first in Africa. On the other hand, the authority of the popular magistrates, of the ancient Republican magistrates, was everywhere restricted by that of the emperor and his delegates. Thus, to confine ourselves to the magistrates with whom the private law is most concerned, the two prætors continued to retain the civil administration of justice. But they found themselves relieved of more and more important fragments of it by imperial agents appointed by the prince at his pleasure, for an indefinite period, such as the prefect of the market, the prefect of the town, the prefect of the watch, the prefect of the *praetorium,*—authorities who were administrative and no longer judiciary, and who, instead of deciding litigations according to the regular forms of the *ordo judiciorum privatorum,* decided them without formality, *extra ordinem,* and applied, in more and more frequent instances, the procedure which had become that of common law since the time of Diocletian.

2.—*The law and its interpreters.*

Precisely by reason of its character as a period of transition, the period of the principate is the one during which the sources of law were most numerous. We find at the same time the sources which existed during the Republic,—enacted law, custom, and edicts, none of which had become entirely exhausted, especially at its commencement,—and certain new sources, the successive activity of which corresponds to the logical development of the imperial authority, first covered in its usurpations by the senate, and afterwards frankly avowed,—namely, the *senatusconsulta,* and the imperial constitutions. Lastly, the period of the principate presents one more source of a very different order, which is merely a strange and temporary manifestation of the influence of the jurisconsults, and the study of which will be taken up in connection with that of their sphere of action, the *responsa prudentium.*

I. **Custom.**—Custom (*usus, mos, consuetudo*) remains during the whole of this period, a source of law in full operation, equally effective for the creation of new law, and the extinguishment of existing law. It is, indeed, a jurist of this period who has given the best definition of the new supplementary role which it filled alongside of the other sources, now that it had ceased to be the only source, and that there had come into existence a written law(*cc*).

II. **Laws.**—The rôle of the legislative *comitia* had almost ceased, as I have said, since the second half of the

(*cc*) Julianus, *D.,* 1, 3, *De leg.,* 32, 1. The opening sentence relates to the creative power of custom; the second assigns as a reason that the silent consent of the people is equivalent to its express consent. The third affirms the abrogatory power of custom. See also Ulpian, *D., h. t.,* 33. Cf. on the two texts, A. Pernice, *Z. S. St.,* 20, 1899, pp. 154-162.

reign of Tiberius. Nevertheless, there were still during this period certain legislative measures relating to private law, the text of some of which has come down to us.

There were produced, under Augustus, a certain number of legislative measures relating to private law which bear his name, and which, therefore, had been proposed by him:—the two *leges Juliae* mentioned by Gaius as having accomplished the suppression of the procedure of the *actiones legis* begun by the *lex Aebutia*, both of which probably belonged to A.U.C. 737 (B.C. 17); the *lex Julia de maritandis ordinibus*, sometimes placed in A.U.C. 757 (A.D. 3), but which in reality belonged to A.U.C. 736 (B.C. 18); the *lex Julia de adulteriis et de fundo dotali*, which probably belongs to A.U.C. 736 (B. C. 18), which, in any case, finds its place before A.U.C. 738 (B.C. 16). There were also some proposed by other magistrates:—the *lex Papia Poppaea*, proposed by the two supplementary consuls of A.U.C. 762 (A.D. 8), which constitutes with the *lex Julia de maritandis ordinibus* the famous system of the caduciary laws; in A.U.C. 757 (A.D. 3), the *lex Aelia Sentia* concerning enfranchisements, proposed by the consuls Sextus Aelius Catus and Caius Sentius; lastly, the *lex Fufia Caninia*, restricting testamentary enfranchisement, which is placed under the reign of Augustus by Suetonius. Under Tiberius, there is scarcely anything to mention except the *lex Junia Vellaea*,—which, if the name has been correctly reported, is a consular law of A.U.C. 779 (A.D. 26),—and perhaps

the law concerning enfranchisements called by Justinian *Junia Norbana,* which in that case must almost necessarily have belonged to the consuls of A.U.C. 772 (A.D.
18), but which the other texts call simply *Junia,* and
which intrinsic evidence leads one rather to place at the
end of the preceding period, between A.U.C. 710 and
A.U.C. 727 (B.C. 44 and B.C. 27). Lastly, among the
laws of Claudius (A.D. 41-54), the most interesting
from the point of view of private law is the *lex Claudia*
upon the guardianship of women.

Among the laws the text of which has reached us directly, the only *lex rogata,* voted by the people on the
proposal of a magistrate, which has been handed down to
us by an inscription, is the law conferring upon Vespasian the tribunitial and certain other powers, the concluding part of which has come to us upon a bronze tablet. We have, moreover, not through an inscription,
but in the treatise upon aqueducts of Frontinus, the text
of another more ancient law, the *lex Quinctia* of A.U.C.
745 (B.C. 9), which is the only law of which we possess
the preamble complete (the *praescriptio*), and the one
which best proves the difference between the laws of the
comitia tributa and plebiscites. But we have, besides that,
a fairly large quantity of *leges datae* made by the emperor
by delegation of the people. I shall only notice here the
tables of Malaga and Salpensa, containing extensive
fragments of the statutory charters given to those Latin
towns by Domitian, between the years A.D. 81 and 84, and

which are as important for the institutions of the Latin towns, as the bronzes of Osuna are for those of the cities composed of citizens; and after them the collection, continually becoming more numerous, of military diplomas, letters of discharge, granting the citizenship to soldiers at the end of their term of service, if they did not already possess it, or, if they did, certain other privileges, and of which each soldier thus honoured used to preserve an extract on a small memorandum formed.of two bronze tablets(*d*).

III. Edicts of the magistrates. (*dd*).—The power of the judiciary magistrates to issue edicts was not directly affected by the establishment of the principate. But, in point of fact, under the new regime, the magistrates lost their independence, and their spirit of initiative, and, whereas the spontaneous innovations of the prætors had been very numerous in the short interval of about a century which separates the *lex Aebutia* from the accession of Augustus, the later prætors only very seldom produced any, and then almost exclusively on the invitation of superior authorities, and, in particular, of the senate.

(*d*) There will be found in my *Textus*, the *lex de imperio Vespasiani*, the *lex Quinctia*, the laws of Malaga and of Salpensa, two examples of military diplomas, and the list of the other *leges datae*. The most complete collection and best commentary on existing military diplomas has been given by Mommsen, *C. I. L.*, III., pp. 843-919, *Suppl.* (1893), pp. 1955-2038, and *Suppl.*, 2, 1902, pp. 2122-2214, 2328, 64-72.

(*dd*) Krueger, *Sources*, § 13. Bruns-Lenel, *Gesch. und Quell.*, § 40.

In the absence of such invitations they contented themselves with reproducing the edicts of their predecessors without adding anything to them, so that their edicts became purely *tralaticia*, without any *pars nova*.

The *de facto* condition of things was given legal effect in the reign of Hadrian, by a reform which the authorities, fairly harmonious on the whole, although belonging to much later times, attribute to the jurisconsult Salvius Julianus, and which had for its object to give a legally definitive form to the edict, already definitive in practice, and to make a precise and official codification of it. But the circumstances and the scope of the reform have, among modern authors, given rise to questions which I must summarily indicate(*e*).

It is certain that the codification was made under Hadrian, and, therefore, between A.D. 117 and A.D. 138(*f*). It is certain also that it was made by Juli-

---

(*e*) The principal documents are two preliminary constitutions of the Digest, *Const. Tanta*, § 18, and *Const.* ωχεν § 18; Victor, *De Caes.*, 19; Eutropius, 8, 17 .

(*f*) The more precise date of A.D. 131 given by St. Jerome's edition of Eusebius, and still defended by C. Ferrini, *Rendiconti dell'Ist. Lombardo*, series 2, vol. 24, fasc. 8, 1891, is, Mommsen has shewn, an arbitrary addition to Eutropius, 8, 17, which is here Jerome's sole authority. Krueger merely holds that the codification was prior to the year 129, when Julianus would seem to have borrowed the order of its arrangement for the first part of his *Digesta*.

anus(*g*), either by virtue of an extraordinary mandate of the emperor, or during his prætorship. (Both are possible, and there is no decisive text.) It is, moreover, certain that the work of Julianus was ratified by a *senatusconsultum*, the effect of which was not, as has sometimes been very loosely stated, to give it the force of law, .—for in that case the distinction between the *jus civile* and the *jus praetorium*, which lasted up to Justinian, would have been obliterated;—but which must have had for its object, conformably with the habit of the senate of addressing instructions to magistrates, to require subsequent magistrates to conform their edicts to the type established by Julianus. Lastly, it is certain that this type was to have application both to the edict of the *praetor urbanus* and to that of the curule ædiles, and that the codification extended to the edict of the ædiles.

On the other hand, there has been keen discussion respecting the questions: 1. Whether the codification extended to the other judiciary magistrates, to the *praetor*

(*g*) There is no occasion, I think, to delay over the assertion made in the Byzantine work of the tenth century, the *Epitome legum* of the year 920, that Julianus had a collaborator named Servius Cornelius, whom Cuq, *Conseil des Empereurs*, 1884, pp. 330-1, has sought to identify with the consul of the year 149, the proconsul of Africa in 153. It is probable that, as has been now for a long time thought, the mention of Servius Cornelius is the result of an amalgamation of the name of the commentator on the edict, Servius Sulpicius (p. 89, n. v), and that of the author of the *lex Cornelia* of A.D. 687 (B.C. 67) (p. 87, n. t.).

peregrinus as well as the *praetor urbanus,* to the governors of provinces as well as the magistrates of Rome;
2. In what measure the reform of Julianus affected
the powers of the magistrates to whom it did relate—
whether, that is to say, the obligation to change nothing
implied that of adding nothing; whether, as some say,
the magistrates could add *clausulae novae*; whether, as
some go so far as to assert, they always had to this extent
the *jus edicendi.* But these questions, in my view, are
the outcome of confusions.

. 1. As to the *jus edicendi,* there can be no doubt that
the magistrate retained it afterwards as before, since the
very thing the reform prescribed for him was to exercise
it in a certain manner. He always posted up his edicts
at the beginning of the year. Gaius still asserts as a present fact, after the reform, that *jus edicendi habent
magistratus populi Romani*(*h*).

But, no less certainly, the system established by the
senatusconsultum was not to be derogated from; for the
compositio edicti had for its very object to hinder these
changes of form. I think it, indeed, very doubtful whether the magistrate could add *clausulae novae* to the
edict; for the two preliminary constitutions of the
Digest, which are our principal source of information,
say that in case of omission or imperfection, one must
henceforth address the emperor. The examples which

(*h*) Gaius, 1, 6.

are cited of *clausulae novae* posterior to Hadrian (*i*), come, in my opinion, from misunderstood texts.

2. As to the different magistrates upon whom the reform was imposed, we must take up the case of the *praetor peregrinus* separately from that of the provincial magistrates, and in both cases avoid confusing distinct questions.

In the case of the *praetor peregrinus* the question arises whether the edict of Julianus imposed upon him a model which he was obliged to follow; and also, whether the reform of Julianus had the effect of combining the two edicts into one sole edict. Now there are here two questions. There is nothing to prove that the edict of the *praetor peregrinus* and that of the *praetor urbanus* were fused under Hadrian; and it is not probable, because there were still at that time in Rome plenty of peregrins, and Gaius speaks always of the two edicts as in active operation. But, on the other hand, Hadrian, when he drew up the edict of the *praetor urbanus,* and by *senatusconsultum* commanded its observance by future prætors, may very probably have done the same thing at the same time for the edict of the *praetor peregrinus* and for future *praetores peregrini*(*j*).

(*i*) See, for example, Cuq, *Conseil des Empereurs*, p. 332, n. 4.

(*j*) There is no necessity to urge to the contrary the lack of information relative to this codification; for this lack of information extends to everything connected with the edict of the *praetor peregrinus,* and is explained by the disappearance of the

A similar and even greater multiplicity of questions suggest themselves in the case of the governors of provinces. Thus these three questions are asked, and often confounded together:—whether the provincial magistrates had lost the *jus edicendi* after Julianus; whether Julianus's reform applied to the provincial edicts; and whether the provincial edicts were replaced by one single provincial edict(*k*). But here, again, several points must be distinguished.

The governors in the provinces, afterwards as before, must have continued to issue an edict upon their entry upon office; thus they always possessed the *jus edicendi*, and each province always had in theory its separate edict.

juridical literature relating to *peregrini* which the concession of the citizenship to all the inhabitants of the Empire brought with it. The only allusions to the edict of the *praetor peregrinus* which have come down to us are found in the *lex Rubria*, c. 20 (*Textes*, p. 66) in Gaius, 4, 37, and perhaps in the citations from Labeo, *libro XXX praetoris peregrini*, made by Ulpian, *D.*, 4, 3, *De dolo*, 9, 4a, where, as a matter of fact, Mommsen considers *praetoris peregrini* as a corruption of *posteriorum*.

(*k*) The question has been principally agitated in reference to the commentary on the provincial edict, written under the Antonines by Gaius, of which the Digest contains numerous extracts, and of which it has been questioned whether he is commenting on an abstract provincial edict or on the concrete edict of a determinate province. See on this subject the authors cited in Karlowa, *R. R. G.*, 1, p. 631 *et seq.*; also Glasson, *Étude sur Gaius*, 2nd ed., 1888, p. 305 *et seq.*

But there is nothing in this to shew that the *senatus-consultum* did not apply to governors as much as to præ-tors; or that it did not order them either to conform to a type settled for each province, or, more probably, to conform in the case of all the provinces, in principle, to a uniform type: from which it would result that, while containing different legal provisions in different places, these edicts would, in fact, reproduce the same model, as, indeed, such model existed to a great extent, from the time of the Republic. The only questions which suggest themselves are the following:—firstly, to what degree the provincial type differed from the urban type; secondly, whether it left absolutely no room for local variation.

I shall close the subject of the edict of Julianus by stating that its general arrangement, at any rate as far as concerns the edict of the *praetor urbanus* and that of the curule ædiles, is now completely restored, thanks to the order followed with virtual unanimity by the principal commentaries, and is in its turn very useful for the understanding of the extracts from it contained in these different commentaries(*l*). It will be sufficient here to

(*l*) The main body of the instrument is furnished by the numerous extracts contained in the Digest from the commentaries on the edict of Paulus and of Ulpian, from Gaius's commentary on the provincial edict and from the first part of the Digest of Julianus. The standard work on the restitution of the edict of Julianus is now the masterly book of Otto Lenel, *Das Edictum perpetuum*, 1883. French transl. in two vols., Paris, 1901-1903. See my review, *N. R. hist.*, 1904, pp. 117-164. Other bibliographical information will be found: *Textes*, p. 117.

indicate the general structure of the two edicts. They both consisted of a principal part, which included both the edicts and the *formulae* of actions, and of an appendix containing *formulae* only. In the edict of the prætor there was at the end an appendix, or rather three appendices containing the *formulae* of interdicts, exceptions, and prætorian stipulations. As to the body of the edict, which preceded it, and comprised the edicts proper and the *formulae of actions*, it was divided into four principal parts. The first and the fourth related, one to the initiation of process up to the delivery of the *formula*, and the other to execution subsequent to judgment. The second and the third, the distinction between which was less exactly marked, contained the edicts and the *formulae* of actions which did not fall within the two former categories, dividing them probably into pleas which were based upon the *jurisdictio* of the magistrate, and into pleas which proceeded from his *imperium*. The whole, main body and appendices, was divided into titles designated by rubrics, and perhaps numbered, in which the different edicts and *formulae* were possibly further grouped under other special rubrics. The edict of the ædiles in like manner commenced with a principal part, containing the edicts proper and the *formulae* of actions, and ended with an appendix, containing the *formula* of an ædilitian stipulation (*m*).

(*m*) Besides the principal work of Lenel, the edicts, the text of which is still extant, will be found collected and restored to

It will be sufficient merely to mention as a sort of resurrection of the *jus edicendi* in its ancient form unexpectedly occurring at the end of the period under consideration, the right, recognised by a constitution of A.D. 235 as belonging to the prefects of the *praetorium*, and still exercised by them in the period subsequent to Diocletian, of promulgating general constitutions, while not derogating either from the statutory law or from the imperial constitutions(*n*).

IV. Senatusconsulta.—The legislative power of the senate was a bridge between that of the *comitia* and that of the emperor. The *comitia* were, as Augustus himself had found by experience, always liable to spasmodic aspirations after independence. The principate was still too recent to permit itself to legislate openly of its own authority. The senate lent it the cover of its name(*o*).

The senate had, from Republican times, begun its encroachments upon the powers of the *comitia* by according dispensations from the laws in case of urgency, or in individual cases. It had also, from Republican times, used its authority over the magistrates by inviting them to realise by the aid of their powers the reforms which it

order in the *Fontes*, pp. 202-230 (restitution of Lenel) and in my *Textes*, pp. 129-150. Moreover, some examples of separate edicts of other magistrates belonging to this period will be found in *Textes*, p. 159 *et seq.*, and *Fontes*, p. 233 *et seq.*

(*n*) Alexander Severus, *C.*, 1, 26, *De off. praef. praet.*, 2. Cf. Krueger, *Sources*, pp. 144, 370, 371.

(*o*) Cf. the remarks of Pomponius, *D.*, 1, 2, *De o. j.*, 2, 9.

judged desirable,—for example, by inviting the prætors to make prætorian laws(*p*). And naturally, when
the imperial authority urged it to assume a more active
legislative rôle, it was again obliged to have recourse to
this last-mentioned procedure. But the senate did not
stop there. It went the length of arrogating to itself the
power of directly making and unmaking *jus civile,* of
precisely filling the place of comitial law. This strictly
legislative power of the senate is attested as early as the
time of Antoninus Pius, by the jurisconsult Gaius(*q*),
who, however, refers to past controversy concerning it.

The only doubtful point is as to how far back the controversy dates, from what period people recognised in
the senate not only the right of inviting the prætor to
make prætorian law, but also that of making *jus civile.*
Many writers consider the controversy as dating from the
time of the Republic, and they invoke in support certain
senatusconsulta, which they hold to attest the right of
the senate from the middle of the first century to make

(*p*) The earliest example is, so far as I know, the *senatusconsultum* of A.U.C. 561 (B.C. 193), prescribing to the praetor
to apply against the Italians usury laws which were aimed only
at citizens (Livy, 35, 7). It was, however, speedily ratified by a
plebiscitum, the *lex Sempronia,* probably because at this time the
praetor could not yet make praetorian law, and the *senatusconsultum* could only operate on ground of urgency (p. 71, n. b.).

.(*q*) Gaius, 1, 4: *Senatusconsultum est quod senatus jubet
atque constituit idque legis .vicem obtinet, quamvis fuerit quae-.
situm.* Cf. Ulpian, *D.,* 1, 3, *De leg.,* 9, who also alludes to the
past controversy, and Papinian, *D.,* 1, 1, *De j. et j.,* 7 *pr.*

jus civile(*r*). In my view, the first certain testimony is found in a *senatusconsultum* of the time of Hadrian, *i.e.*, the *Sc. Tertullianum,* on the right of succession of the mother, and it is very possible that the senate up to that time achieved the realisation of its legislative reforms by way of injunction to the magistrates. This agrees perfectly with the consultative, and not imperative, language which it continued to employ, and especially with the simply prætorian effect of the three most important *senatusconsulta* of this period relating to private law(*s*).

The legislative power of the senate, when once recognised as incontestible, was not exercised by it for very long. The *senatusconsultum* was little by little superseded as a source of law by an evolution which made the adhesion of the senate to what was proposed to it something certain and compulsory, and which consequently by degrees put in the place of the *senatusconsultum,*—of the resolution of the senate, which was in ancient time alone important,—the statement of grounds for legislation, originally devoid of all importance, but which

(*r*) Lenel, *Ursprung und Wirkung der Exceptionen,* 1876, p. 49 *et seq.*, invokes in this sense the provisions of the *senatusconsulta* relating to the houses purchased by removers of old buildings (*Textes,* p. 124 *et seq.*), and some *senatusconsulta* cited *D.,* 38, 4, *Dc ads. lib.,* 1 *pr.,* and *D.,* 40, 5, *De fid. lib.,* 51, 4, which do not in my opinion prove the point, excepting to people who are already convinced.

(*s*) *Sc. Velleianum* of A.D. 46; *Sc. Trebellianum* of A.D. 55 or 56; *Sc. Macedonianum* of the time of Vespasian (69-79).

later on was always approved, and consequently became the essential matter. This transformation attached to the *senatusconsulta* proposed by the emperor, to the *orationes principis in senatu habitae*. The imperial proposals, which had become the most important, which perhaps were the only ones after Hadrian(*t*), were in fact always given effect. It was, therefore, natural that, after a certain date, about the end of the second century, the jurisconsults themselves frankly adopted the significant habit, long before introduced into popular language, of citing in place of the *senatusconsulta*, the orations of which they were no more than the inevitable corollaries (*oratio Severi*, of A.D. 195; *oratio Antonini*, of A.D. 206). And thus, moreover, it is easy to understand why the authors of these *orationes* came more and more to use the open language of command in place of a conventional parliamentary mode of speech(*u*). But, from the day when this state of feeling existed between the governors and the governed, there was no longer any reason to have recourse to a fiction which neither deceived nor aimed at deceiving anybody. We find no more *senatusconsulta* of a legislative character after the commencement of the third century.

The *senatusconsulta* were designated by the texts, not formally, as laws were, by the proper name of their author, or of their authors, expressed in the femi-

---

(*t*) See Krueger, p. 113, note 3.

(*u*) See for example the *Oratio Severi, D., 27, 9, De reb. eor.,* 1, 2: *Praeterea, patres conscripti, interdicam.*

nine (*lex Aelia Sentia*), but in a manner merely popular, by an adjective generally derived from the name of one of the consuls under whose consulate they were issued(*v*) (*Sc. Trebellianum*, issued *Trebellio Maximo et Annaeo Seneca consulibus*). The inscriptions have preserved some of these, amongst which the latest is a *senatusconsultum* of A.D. 176 or 177, restricting the expenses of the gladiatorial games. But we are most interested in those which relate to private law, and of several of these the text has been transmitted completely or partially, either by inscriptions, or more especially by the Digest(*w*). I shall only cite, after the *senatusconsultum* concerning quasi-usufruct,

(*v*) And not, as is almost unanimously said, of the consuls who proposed them. See, for example, for the *Sc. Trebellianum*, Gaius, 2, 253: *Trebellio Maximo et Annaeo Seneca consulibus senatusconsultum factum est*, compared with 2, 255, 256: *Ex senatu consulto Trebelliano . . . ex Trebelliano senatusconsulto;* and for the *Sc. Pegasianum*, Gaius, 2, 254, compared with 2, 256. We have there, these witnesses shew, only an abbreviation of the citation of the *senatusconsulta* by their consular date, of which there are many other examples (Gaius, 3, 63. Ulpian, *D.*, 40, 5, *De fid. lib.*, 26, 7, 28, 4. Venuleius, *D.*, 48, 8, *Ad leg. Corn. de sic.*, 6). But this practice having nothing official about it, the denomination of a *senatusconsultum* might be equally taken from the name of the person whose conduct had provoked it, as in the case of the *Sc. Macedonianum*, and especially from that of the emperor who had inspired it, as in the case of the *Sc. Claudianum* and *Neronianum* voted *Claudio auctore* and *Nerone auctore*.

(*w*) See the enumeration, *Textes*, p. 120, and the *Sc. Hosidianum and Volusianum*, p. 124.

(which belongs to the last years of the Republic or to the very beginning of the Empire), in the first century: (1) under Claudius, the *Sc. Velleianum* of A.D. 46, about women becoming sureties for others; the *Sc. Claudianum* of A.D. 52, about free women who had relation with a slave of another in spite of the prohibition of the master; between A.D. 44 and A.D. 46, the *Sc. Hosidianum* about sales of houses to removers of old buildings, modified under Nero in A.D. 56 by the *Sc. Volusianum*: (2) under Nero (A.D. 54-68), the *Sc. Neronianum*, about legacies void by reason of the formula employed; one or more *senatusconsulta* about the formal drawing up of legal documents in transactions *inter vivos* and of wills, of which one at least belongs to A.D. 61; in A.D. 55 or 56, the *Sc. Trebellianum*, about *fideicommissa*, followed (3) under Vespasian (A.D. 69-79), by the *Sc. Pegasianum;* again under Vespasian, the *Sc. Macedonianum* concerning the loaning of money to sons *in potestate*. In the second century I shall cite: (1) under Hadrian (A.D. 117-138), the *Sc. Juventianum* of A.D. 129, about *petitio hereditatis,* and the *Sc. Tertullianum,* about succession of mother to children; (2) under Marcus Aurelius, the *Sc. Orfitianum*, of A.D. 178, about the succession of child to mother; then (3) the *oratio Severi* of A.D. 195, about the alienation of the property of minors, and (4) the *oratio Antonini* of A.D. 206, about donations between husband and wife, which end the list.

V. Imperial Constitutions(x).—By the time the senate left off making laws, this power had long since passed to the emperor. The ordinances of the emperors (*constitutiones principum*) are mentioned by Gaius, in the time of Antoninus Pius, without distinction of kind, as having the force of law, and he even says of them, contrasting them, in this respect, with *senatusconsulta*, that their legislative authority, based on the law of investiture, had never been contested(y). We must, nevertheless, distinguish their different kinds, and define their respective authority, which was not at all times the same.

Gaius indicates three kinds of *constitutiones principum*:—the *edicta*, the *epistulae*—or rather the *rescripta*, which in stricter terminology are sometimes divided into *epistulae* and *subscriptiones*—and the *decreta*(z). A fourth is habitually added—the *mandata*. The *edicta* are edicts corresponding to those of the magistrates, and posted up as they were, *in albo*. The *mandata* were individual instructions addressed to determinate functionaries, which Gaius and Ulpian omit, perhaps intentionally because of their administrative character, but which

(x) Krueger, *Sources*, § 14. Bruns-Lenel, *Gesch. und Quell.*, §§ 41-45. Mommsen, *Dr. Publ.*, 5, p. 1.5 *et seq.*

(y) Gaius, 1, 5: *Constitutio principis, est quod imperator decreto vel edicto vel epistula constituit. Nee umquam dubitatum est, quin id legis vicem optineat, cum ipse imperator per legem imperium accipiat.* Cf. Pomponius, *D.*, 1, 2, *De o. j.*, 2, 11, 12. Ulpian, *D.*, 1, 4, *De const. princ.*, 1, *pr.*

(z) Gaius, 1, 5. Cf. Ulpian, *D.*, 1, 4, *De const. prin.*, 1, 1.

nevertheless introduced some rules of law. The *decreta* were judgments delivered by the emperor, either on appeal or of first instance, by virtue of his right of summoning the parties before himself. Lastly, the rescripts were answers made by the emperor on points of law to magistrates or to private persons; they were habitually transcribed at the foot of the case submitted by the private person (*subscriptiones*), in order that the answer might not be separated from the question, but were sent in the form of separate letters (*epistulae*) to the magistrates, against whom it was unnecessary to take the same precaution. We meet with only a few down to the time of Hadrian; but they multiply very much after his reign, probably in consequence of the codification of the edict, and of the invitation then made to magistrates and to pleaders to consult the emperor on doubtful points, which must have caused more of them to be issued, and perhaps, also, in consequence of the system of publication introduced at this period, which must have better insured their preservation.

Their authority ought logically to be different in the different categories, and this was in fact the system which seems to have been in operation at first.

The mandates were individual instructions given to a governor. These instructions only existed for him, and did not apply to his successor, or to the governors of neighbouring provinces, unless also given to them individually, just as was the case, as we have seen, with the provisions of the edict of the magistrates, which, although perhaps the same for several years and in several provinces, existed each year and in each province only on the condition that it had been promulgated by the magistrate for the time being and for the place.

The edicts of the emperor were rules obligatory upon the whole empire, since his authority, direct or indirect, extended all over the realm—instead of being limited to a definite area, as was that of the magistrates of the Republic—and they were obligatory during the whole of his life, instead of being so only for one year, inasmuch as his powers were life-long, instead of being annual. But, logically, they must originally have lost their force on the death of their author(*a*).

The *decreta* were judgments which were imposed upon the parties, but upon the parties only, by virtue of rules relating to the authority of *res judicatae*.

Lastly, the rescripts were opinions very analogous to the *responsa prudentium*. They were imposed upon the judge of the matter for the purpose for which they were obtained, as we shall see was the case also with the *responsa* (p. 145). They were also the origin of a special procedure, the procedure by way of rescript, in which

---

(*a*) This is, I believe, the reason why the same rule is sometimes mentioned as having been issued by successive edicts of different emperors. See, for example, on the edicts of Augustus and Claudius, who had, before the *Sc. Velleianum*, forbidden women to become surety for their husband: *D.*, 16, 1, *Ad Sc. Vell.*, 2, *pr*.

the conditional rescript delivered by the imperial chancellery took the place of the *formula*, and which, as early as the second century, constituted another blow to the formulary procedure(*b*). But rescripts delivered upon a concrete case had not the force of law for similar or analogous cases, any more than *responsa prudentium*.

There is a decisive reason why neither the rescripts nor the other imperial constitutions could have had the force of definitive and general law at the commencement of the empire; for that would presuppose in the emperor himself a legislative power which he did not in any wise possess at that time. Legislative power, apart from the case of the *leges datae* (p. 108), did not result from any of the jurisdictions which had been conferred upon him. If he possessed it, it would be impossible to explain in what sense the *cura legum et morum*, intended to confer it upon him, could have been on three separate occasions offered to Augustus and refused by him(*c*). Lastly, if he possessed it, it is incomprehensible how he could have been himself subject in principle to the ordinary laws, and have needed to obtain special exemptions from them, for example from the caduciary laws (p. 107), the *jus patrum*, which was conceded to several of the first emperors by the senate(*d*).

(*b*) See notably on this procedure, Puchta, *Inst.*, § 178. Baron, *Inst.*, p. 451. Pernice, *Festgabe für Bescler*, 1885, p. 51 *et seq.=Archivio*, 36, 1886, p. 33 *et seq.*

(*c*) *Mon. Ancyr.*, 3, 14 *et seq.* See Mommsen, *Dr. publ.*, 4, p. 430, n. 1.

(*d*) Mommsen, *Dr. publ.*, 5, p. 166, n. 1.

But as the empire continued, the ideas on the subject became modified. From the time of Vespasian, the emperor conceded the *jus patrum* instead of receiving it(*e*). He was soon looked upon as being, as a general rule, above the law. And not only Gaius, but Pomponius also, as early as the time of Hadrian, recognised in him the legislative power, by virtue of a provision of the law of investiture, which certainly had not this meaning, but to which it was thenceforth attributed; and,—I believe, in spite of numerous attempts at limitation made by modern authorities,—legislative power from every point of view, both in respect to the right to make new law, and in respect to the right to interpret the law, and as much by one species of constitution as by another.

The only restriction, which principally had to do with rescripts and decrees, resulted from the will of the prince, and consequently was not a true restriction at all. His decisions naturally had only the scope which he wished to give them. He might in a rescript, or in a decree, establish a new rule, meaning it to govern all future cases. He might, on the contrary, mean only to deal with the particular case with which he was seized. Such was the case when, as the texts express it, he delivered a *constitutio personalis*. Such was the case, also, in the very numerous instances in which he only applied existing law, without any intention to innovate, even although he might incidentally touch some controverted point. In

(*e*) Mommsen, *Dr. publ.*, 5, p. 166, n. 2.

truth the distinction seems to have been anything but clear, and it must have been one difficult to make in practice. A document recently discovered seems to establish that this distinction was marked very definitely by a concrete fact: certain decrees and rescripts were officially published at Rome by posting up, while others were. sent direct to the demandant. The will of the emperor was no doubt considered as manifesting itself by the employment of the one or of the other procedure. The rescripts special to the business in hand were those sent to the applicant, as they all were at first; the ones which had legislative force were those which were posted up like the edicts, following a usage which probably dates from the time of Hadrian, and which the new text—a constitution of Gordian discovered at Scaptoparena in Thrace—proves to have existed under Gordian, A.D. 238(f).

There have come down to us at first hand certain imperial constitutions of the period of the principate(g):

(f) Text and discussions, *Textes*, p. 188 *et seq.* It is Mommsen who is entitled to the honour of having brought out the exceptional importance of this document. See, in the contrary sense, Krueger, p. 128, n. 7. I pass over here altogether the subject of the work of juridical deliberation, and of the practical drawing up of the different imperial constitutions. See on this subject Krueger, p. 142 *et seq.* and the references.

(g) *Textes*, p. 169 *et seq.* There may be mentioned, although necessarily it is not up to date, Haenel's book, *Corpus legum ab imperatoribus Romanis ante Justinianum latarum*, 1857, which gives, for this period and the following, all the extant imperial constitutions not included in the compilations, and also general

for example, an edict of Claudius of the year 46, giving or confirming the right of citizenship to the people of the neighbourhood of Trent, found at Cles in 1869; a constitution of Hadrian upon the rights of succession of the children of soldiers, the Greek version of which has been preserved for us by one of the Berlin papyri; a rescript of Commodus in answer to the complaints of colonists against the administrators of the imperial domains, discovered in Africa in 1880; and again the above cited constitution of Scaptoparena. There exists a much larger number of them in the official or private collections of the period after Diocletian.

V. **The science of law and the responsa prudentium.** The history of the science of law in this period (*h*), which

tables of the constitutions of the codes, by their dates, names of persons and names of places, &c.

(*h*) See, on the general subject, the work of Krueger, §§ 18-27, which renders it almost needless to resort, for the biography of the jurisconsults, to the more ancient literature. On the other hand it is very easy and very profitable to seek out, in the *Palingenesia* of Lenel, the texts which have come down to us from each jurisconsult. Some information also about the life of the jurisconsults and the chronological succession of their works will be found in the notices which precede, in my *Textes*, the fragments of Pomponius, Gaius, Papinian, Paulus, Ulpian and Modestinus. Lastly we may also resort to the notices of the *Prosopographia imperii Romani saec. I., II., III.*, 3 vols. in quarto, 1897-1898; for the jurisconsults of the period from Augustus to Hadrian, to vol. II of the *Jurisprudentia antehadriana* of Bremer; and for the jurisconsults of the time of Augustus and Tiberius, to Bremer, *Jurisprudentia antehadriana*, 2, 1, 1898.

is the most brilliant one, and which at least up to the death of Alexander Severus, constitutes what is called the period of the classical jurists, opens by an event, at the same time very well known and very obscure:—the division of the jurisconsults into two sects, or two schools: one founded by Labeo, whose successor was Proculus, whence the name Proculians, and the other by Capito, whose successor was Masurius Sabinus, whence the name Sabinians(i).

M. Antistius Labeo, who was sprung from an old plebeian family, and the son of a jurisconsult who served the Republic at Philippi, and killed himself after that defeat, remained under Augustus openly attached to the ancient institutions, and refused the consulate after having held the prætorship(j). His adversary, C. Ateius Capito, recognises his juridical power, but accuses him of having an excessive spirit of independence. Tacitus relates, on the other hand, that the servility of Capito was so great that while it gained for him the favours of Augustus and of Tiberius, it attracted also universal contempt. We may, however, ask whether it is not due to a classical taste for symmetry that people have opposed the one man to the other; for while the traces of Labeo in subsequent literature are conspicuously and deeply

(i) Pomponius D., 1, 2, De o. j., 2, 47-53. See, lastly, G. Baviera Le due scuole dei giureconsulti romani, 1898.

(j) The Labeo of Pernice, 1, pp. 7-92, commences with a detailed biography of Labeo.

marked, the citations from Capito are few and far between, and one may say that none of them have reference to private law.

After them there are mentioned as having been at the head of the two groups, from the reign of Tiberius almost up to that of Hadrian, different jurisconsults, of whom the principal are:—for the Proculians, Proculus, the two Nervas, Pegasus, Neratius and the two Celsi, the second of whom, the son, consul in A.D. 129 for the second time, was one of the most vigorous and original of the Roman jurisconsults; for the Sabinians, the two Sabini, Masurius and Caelius, between whom comes C. Cassius Longinus, consul in A.D. 30—from whom the sect sometimes takes the name of Cassiani, and who shews that the political disagreements of Labeo and Capito had no influence upon the subsequent destinies of the two schools, for he was a descendant of the murderer of Caesar, and was exiled in the time of Nero because of the reverence which he shewed for the memory of his ancestor; then Javolenus who occupied high positions under Domitian and Trajan(k); and lastly, Salvius Julianus, the author of the codification of the edict, the contemporary and rival of Celsus, one of the most important of the jurisconsults, and one of those from whom subsequent literature contains most citations(l).

(k) See N. R. hist., 1894, p. 556, a new inscription relating to the political career of Javolenus.

(l) The book of H. Buhl, Salvius Julianus, 1, 1886, opens with an extended biography of Julianus. A shorter notice is

It is generally admitted that Pomponius, who gives this enumeration, must have been himself a Sabinian. The distinction between the two sects is not subsequently mentioned as in any way a live subject, excepting by Gaius, the contemporary of Antoninus Pius and of Marcus Aurelius, who calls the Sabinians his masters (*praeceptores nostri*), but who, I believe, lived in the provinces,

devoted to him, *Prosopographia, III.*, pp. 164-165, no. 102. It is now necessary to rectify and supplement both of them by the help of an important inscription discovered in 1899 in Tunis, which has been published and commented on especially by Jauckler, *Comptes Rendus de l'Académie des Inscriptions*, 1899, pp. 366-374, Boulard, *L. Salvius Julianus*, Thesis, Paris, 1902, pp. 9-20, and Mommsen, *Z.S. St.* 23, 1902, pp. 9-20. This inscription was certainly dedicated to the jurisconsult Julianus, of whom it relates that he was from the time of his quaestorship, the object of the exceptional favour of Hadrian, *propter insignem doctrinam*, and it makes known for the first time his complete names and his political career up to the proconsulate of Africa, held by him after the accession of Marcus Aurelius, and of L. Verus. The prenomen of *L(ucius)*, which it gives to him seems to refute the opinion of Borghesi, followed by Cuq, *Conseil des Empereurs*, p. 341, n. 3, which would identify him with the consul of the year 148, Salvius Julianus, named *P(ublius)* according to the copy of an inscription no longer extant. But the chronological data furnished by the new inscription lead one to place the consulate of the jurisconsult at approximately the same date, and Mommsen, who had previously disputed Borghesi's identification, has admitted that it follows from this inscription, concluding that it is in the copy of the other inscription that the prenomen of the consul of 148 has been incorrectly stated.

and probably there followed an antiquated usage already become out of fashion in the capital(*m*).

A singular fact is the obscurity which exists both as to the theoretical character of the disagreements between the two groups, and as to the positive form which their separation took. As to the former, Pomponius maintains that the difference consisted in the spirit of greater or less rigid adherence to precedent marking their doctrines(*n*); but this is only moderately justified by the generality of the controversies which are known to us, and which are, moreover, much less numerous than people often admit, fancying they see school controversies in all the texts in which the leader of a school is cited(*o*). As to the material form of the separation, the manner in which Pomponius sets forth the succession of the jurisconsults at the head of the sects suggests the management of two teaching establishments, of two *stationes publice docentium*(*p*), such as began to exist

(*m*) See for his biography the notice in my *Textes*, p. 176 *et seq;* also an exposure and refutation of a recent theory which would identify him with the jurisconsult of the first century Gaius Cassius Longinus, in N. Herzen, *Z.S. St.* 20, 1899, pp. 211-229.

(*n*) Pomponius, *D.*, 1, 2, *De o. j.*, 2, 47: *Nam Ateius Capito in his quae ei tradita fuerant, perseverabat; Labeo, ingenui qualitate et fiducia doctrinae, qui et ceteris operis sapientiae operam dederat, plurima innovare instituit.*

(*o*) There is a good critical enumeration in Krueger, *Sources*, p. 197, n. 1; and a detailed discussion in G. Baviera, pp. 38-119.

(*p*) Aulus Gellius, 13, 3: *In plerisque Romae stationibus jus publice docentium aut respondentium.* See on the teaching of law, Krueger, *Sources*, p. 189 *et seq.;* Pernice, *Gesch. und Quell.,* § 19.

at this epoch for giving systematic instruction side by side with the purely practical teaching of the preceding period (*q*). Nevertheless, this theory is not free from difficulties; thus, for example, we find in the lists of the heads of the two schools a very large proportion of political personages whom one cannot easily imagine taking the direction of a private school on the disappearance of their predecessors.

Whatever may have been its material form and its theoretical range, the distinction between the two schools scarcely lasted beyond the time of Hadrian. The later jurisconsults of the second century and of the beginning of the third century, who are very considerable in number, are classed in neither. I shall cite among them: the contemporary of Antoninus Pius, Sextus Cæcilius Africanus, a pupil of Julianus(*r*); the contemporary of Antoninus and of Marcus Aurelius, Ulpius Marcellus; Q. Cervidius Scaevola, a somewhat later jurisconsult of

(*q*) Cf. Krueger, *Sources*, p. 184 *et seq.;* Pernice, *Gesch. und Quell.*, p. 134, note 3.

(*r*) The *Quaestiones* of Africanus, his best known work, are, as the Greek commentators and our old writers saw, principally a collection of the decisions of Julianus. It is to Julianus that Africanus' citations refer, not only when he names him, but, in more numerous places where he simply writes '*ait*,' '*putat*,' '*inquit*,' '*respondit*' only, leaving his name unexpressed; and the question arises whether he is not still giving the opinion of Julianus in other places, where he seems to speak for himself and where some such word as 'inquit' may have disappeared. See Buhl, *Salvius Julianus*, 1, pp. 67-85. Cf. P. Krueger, *Sources*, p. 23β, n. 1 and the references.

the same century; and, passing over many other names, the three celebrated jurisconsults of the time of the Severan Emperors, Papinian, Paulus, and Ulpian. Aemilius Papinianus, who is usually considered as the chief of the Roman jurisconsults, was prefect of the *praetorium* under Septimius Severus, and slain by order of Caracalla in A.D. 212 or 213, because he was not willing to pronounce an eulogy on the murder of Geta. Paulus and Ulpian, who were, like him, public functionaries and jurisconsults, and who, moreover, have left many more writings than he has, were both his assessors during his prefectorship of the *praetorium*, and afterwards themselves prefects of the *praetorium* under Alexander Severus. Neither the date of the death of Paulus nor the chronology of his works is very well known. Ulpian seems to have written almost all his works while he was in disgrace under Caracalla (A.D. 212-217), and he was slain by the prætorians in A.D. 228. By reason of the extent and lucidity of his writings he furnished one-third of the Digest, and he is often considered as being, with Papinian and Paulus, one of the three greatest Roman jurisconsults, and almost the equal of Papinian. He is at bottom chiefly a lucid and intelligent compiler, but a little hasty, and very inferior to the creative jurisconsults of the end of the Republic and the first centuries of the Empire(*s*).

(*s*) A. Pernice, *Ulpian als Schriftsteller, Sitzungsberichte* of Berlin, 1885, 1, p. 443, *et seq.* Cf. Krueger, pp. 297.288, n. 3, 443, n. 2.

After Papinian, Paulus, and Ulpian, the series of jurisconsults comes to an end rather abruptly with Herennius Modestinus, prefect of the night guards between A.D. 226 and 244, who is sometimes called the last of the classical jurisconsults. After him we meet with no writers of more than secondary rank, amongst whom I shall only name, as the most recent of those who were put under contribution by the Digest, the two jurisconsults, of uncertain date, Hermogenianus and Arcadius Charisius.

The works of these jurisconsults, which relate almost exclusively to private law, to penal law, and to procedure, and in which public law, properly so called, is but little represented, may, in spite of their diversities, be distributed under certain categories(*t*) :—

1st, The collections of opinions delivered by the jurisconsults in the presence of their pupils, or in answer to their pupils, a usage which dated from the Republic, and continued into the Empire. 2nd, The commentaries on the edict, *libri ad edictum,* studying successively the different matters relating to the edicts and the *formulae* which the *album* contained. 3rd, Along with these the works on the civil law, treating not exactly of all matters of civil law, but of those which had not been already studied in connection with the *formulae* of civil actions in the commentaries on the edict, and for which the systematic arrangement settled by Q. Mucius Scaevola was adopted with certain modifications by Masur-

(*t*) See Krueger, *Sources,* p. 172 *et seq.*

ius Sabinus in his three books on the *jus civile*, which themselves were the foundation of later *libri ad Sabinum*(*u*). 4th, What may be called encyclopedias (*digesta*) treating of all these matters, and also certain others, in a first part corresponding to the commentaries on the edict, and a second part corresponding to the treatises on civil law, following a composite plan which was observed not only in all the treatises of the same character, (for example, in the *digesta* of Celsus and of Julianus), but also in the collections of decisions of cases, such as the Questions and the Responses of Papinian, and in the manuals, such as the Sentences of Paulus. 5th, Elementary didactical works, *institutiones, regulae, enchiridia*(*v*), comprising a systematic exposition of matters of law without distinction between prætorian part and civil part. 6th, and lastly, a number of very miscellaneous monographs on law, as for example, on the functions of particular magistrates.

The sum total of all these works, or, to put it more generally, the complete collection of the works

(*u*) Lenel, *Das Sabinussystem*, 1892, Cf. Krueger, p. 200.

(*v*) It is one of the two works which Pomponius published under this title, his *liber singularis enchiridii*, written under Hadrian, which contained by way of introduction the short history of the sources, magistracies, and jurisconsults, preserved in the long fragment *D.*, 1, 2, *De o. j.*, 2, which remains our richest source of information on the history of the law of the Republic. On the theory of Sanio, *Varroniana in den Schriften der römischen Juristen*, 1867, followed by Krueger, who there considers Varro to have been his principal source, see *N.R. hist.*, 1890, p. 334.

of the jurisconsults of Rome, certainly presented a
more modest bulk than we should be led to suppose by
what we are accustomed to in these days, when the cheap-
ness of raw material and the facilities of mechanical
manufacture make books much less costly. Nevertheless,
its extent has often been too much underrated owing to
a misunderstood statement of Justinian, who says that
the writings placed under contribution by the Digest
were reduced to a twentieth part(w). The conclusion has
been drawn that all the juridical literature of Rome
would be only twenty times the volume of the Digest,—
not even equalling the least of our repertories of law.
But Justinian only speaks of the books of which the compilers took cognisance. We have a surer source of information, the only scientific one, in the number of the
libri of the different works(x). Notwithstanding a
natural attempt to make them coincident with the divisions of subjects, the *libri* approximate to a constant aver-
age size, namely that of the scrolls of papyrus (*volumina*)
on which they were written. Now, on adding them up, one
sees that Justinian's computation is much too moderate.
The works of three or four of the most prolific juriscon-

(w) D. Const. *Tanta*, 1, 1; const. Δεδωχεν 1.

(x) See Krueger, *Sources*, p. 183, and more particularly the
special article by the same author, *Z.S. St.*, 8, 1887, p. 76 *et seq.*,
on the employment of papyrus and parchment in juridical literature, wherein he also shews how we can by the same process,
measure the extent of the gaps in what has come down to us, and
prove, for example, that we possess almost complete such or such
book of Ulpian *ad edictum.*

sults,—for example, Labeo, Pomponius, Paulus, and Ul-
pain,—would be sufficient to exceed it(y).

There has come down to us only a very small fraction
of this literature. The most numerous fragments have
been transmitted to us in an indirect manner, principally
by Justinian's Digest, where the extracts are accompanied by references to the author, the work, and the
book, but with omissions and changes intended to fit them
to the law of the time. This is what constitutes the great
value of the rare fragments which have come down to us
in an independent manner, the most important of which
are:—1. The *Institutiones* of Gaius, a work in four
books, written about A.D. 161, combining in a unique
arrangement the civil law and the prætorian law, which
the author treats of, after some theories about the sources,
under the tripartite division of the law of persons, the
law of things, and the law of actions, following a plan
which has long been believed to be of his own invention,
but which is certainly more ancient. A summary of the
Institutes of Gaius was inserted in the *Lex Romana Visigothorum,* but some complete copies of the original work
were still in existence in the fifth century, and one of them
has come to light again in our time. The parchment had
been scraped in the sixth century to receive a copy of the
epistulae and the *polemica* of St. Jerome; and under this
form it reached the library of the chapter of Verona,
where the text of Gaius was discovered on it by the historian Niebuhr in 1816. Three leaves are missing, and

(y) Pernice, *Gesch. und Quell.,* p. 138, n. 2.

many passages remain illegible. The latest revision of it was made by Studemund, who gave us in 1874 an entire facimile of it, to which was afterwards added supplementary information published for the first time in 1884, at the commencement of the second edition of volume 1 of the *Collectio librorum juris antejustiniani* (*yy*). The four books of Gaius are divided in the different editions into paragraphs.—2. The *Regulae* of Ulpian, (written by him, in the time of Caracalla, on the same plan as the Institutes of Gaius), of which a manuscript, written in Gaul in the tenth century, or at the end of the ninth century, and utilised for the printed copy in the fourteenth century, and afterwards lost and refound in our time in the Vatican, in the collection of Queen Christina, contains a summary divided into titles, and, in the different editions, into paragraphs.—3rd. The *Sententiae* of Paulus, a manual written by him about the year 212, following the plan of the *digesta* and divided into books and titles, to which the editors have

---

(*yy*) There was a momentary hope of possessing a second copy of the Institutes of Gaius in another palimpsest discovered at Autun in 1898 by Emile Chatelain. But, when deciphered, the text, which seems to have been written about the middle of the fifth century, and which was scraped in the seventh century to make room for a copy of the *Institutiones* of Cassianus, was found to give only a sort of academic paraphrase of the Institutes of Gaius, from which, however, some useful information may be derived. It is reproduced at pp. 333-349 of my *Textes*, where there will be found, at p. 205, a list of the principal works having. references to it (see now, also, P. Krueger, *Z.S. St.*, 34, 1903, pp. 375-408).

added paragraphs, which I here cite from direct, although they have come down to us only through the intermediary of the *Lex Romana Visigothorum*. This law only contains an abridgment, but the text has been in part completed from other sources, and also from certain manuscripts of the law of the Visigoths, the copyists of which still possessed a complete text of Paulus, and added some passages from it, both in the body of the law and at the end(z).

(z) I refer for more ample details to the notices in my *Textes*. I refer also to them for some other less important documents of this period, particularly for the Paris and Berlin fragments of Papinian, for the *fragmentum de formulâ Fabianâ*, the Vienna fragment of the Institutes of Ulpian, the Berlin fragment *de judiciis*, and the *fragmentum de jure fisci*; and I further invite attention, as documents discovered since their publication in June, 1903, to a little Heidelberg papyrus relating to the *quarta legitima* published by Gerhard and Grademvitz, *Neue Heidelberger Jahrbücher*, 12, 1903, pp. 141-183, and some parchments at Strasburg containing some fragments of the Disputations of Ulpian, published by Lenel, Berlin *Sitzungsberichte*, 1903, pp. 922-926, 1034-1035; 1904, pp. 1156-1172. There still remains to be mentioned, in order to give a complete list of the documents in which the law of the period may be studied; 1st, The information furnished by non-juridical authors; 2ndly, the actual legal documents which have come down to us. I can only pretend to give very summary hints upon the two points.—1st. As to the literary sources, we find, to begin with, in the period of the principate, historians such as Livy and Dionysius, who might appear to form a very rich mine of information about the political and private institutions of the early period. But, the real value of this information is much below its apparent value. For the first four centuries and also in part for later times, they have borrowed

To complete the history of the jurisconsults and their works, it remains to define the sense in which they were called to participate in legislative power, the sense in

without discrimination from the mass of clumsy fables and conscious falsifications collected by the annalists of the time of Sulla. To deal with them scientifically involves a work of sifting which is far from being completely accomplished. It is quite otherwise with the historical evidence given in reference to the imperial period by authors contemporary or nearly so, such as Tacitus, Suetonius and Dion Cassius, amongst whom the richest in information on private law is Suetonius. It is right to mention also as furnishing much sound information upon the preceding period, the fragments which have come down to us of a collection of abbreviations of the grammarian of the first century, Valerius Probus (*Textes*, p. 169 *et seq.*), and of the dictionary published in the reign of Augustus by Verrius Flaccus, an abridgment of which, made in the second or third century by Festus, is preserved partly in the original, partly in the new abridgment of Paul Diacre (edition of the juridical terms by Mommsen, in Bruns, *Fontes*, 2, pp. 1-98). In pure literature there must be noticed especially the collection of anecdotes composed by Valerius Maximus from trustworthy original sources; the works of Quintilian, where, amid a great deal of rubbish, there is some valuable information derived from his judiciary practice; the *Noctes Atticae* of Aulus Gellius; the *Natural History* of Pliny the elder; and the letters of Pliny the younger. The collection of *agrimensores* (edition and commentary by Lachmann, Rudorff, Blume and Mommsen, *Die Schriften der römischen Feldmesser*, 2 vols., 1848-1852; extracts in Bruns, pp. 88-95) is also very important on the subject of the management of landed property. 2ndly, As to legal documents, we possess for the period under consideration, practical precedents of almost all legal transactions, which have come down to us either in the form of separate documents, or in the two collections of the vouchers and receipts of the Pompeian banker, L. Caecilius Jucundus, in the first century, and in the second, of the triptychs of Transylvania (methodical classifica-

which the *responsa prudentium* were counted among the sources of the law.

tion and principal examples, *Textes*, pp. 721-793; and for the Pompeiian documents, the new edition issued by Zangemeister in 1898, *C. I. L., IV., Suppl.*, 1, and Erman's article, *Z. S. St.*, 20, 1899, pp. 172-211). The Greek-Egyptian papyri have also preserved many Roman legal documents translated into Greek, of all periods. See especially on those at Berlin, Dareste, *N. R. hist.*, 1894, pp. 685-696, and Mitteis, *Hermes*, 30, 1895, pp. 564-618; 33, 1897, pp. 629-659; on those at Oxyrhynchus, Mitteis, *Hermes*, 34, 1899, pp. 88-106; *Archiv für Papyrusforschung*, 1, 1900, pp. 178-199, 343-354; on both of them, O. Gradenwitz, *Einführung in die Papyruskunde*, 1, 1900. Cf. also for the Ostrakas from the same source, U. Wilcken, *Griechische Ostraka aus Aegypten und Nubien*, 2 vols., 1899. However, it is perhaps the two first cited collections which best make known to us the wording, and especially the material form, of Roman deeds of the best period. As to the material form, under the provisions of a *senatusconsultum* of the time of Nero (Paulus, *Sent.*, 5, 25; Suetonius, *Ner.*, 17), which Jucundus' vouchers enable us to place under the year 61 (Zangemeister, *C. I. L., IV., Suppl.*, p. 278), they are written in duplicate on tablets coated with wax (*tabulae*) joined together in book form (*codex*) and divided into one closed part containing the text of the first original, and one open part containing that of the second, and the seals of the witnesses and of those concerned (save in the case of wills regulated differently, or by a different *senatusconsultum* of the same reign, Suetonius, *Ner.*, 17, in the case of which the closed part contains the disposing clauses, and the open part only the name of the testator and the seals). As to the wording, these are all documents available as *primâ facie* evidence. But there were two successive forms of them. Whilst they began by being simple memoranda written by the beneficiary in the transaction, and at most intended to give precision to his recollections, and those of the witnesses, they afterwards became valid acknowledgments emanating from the party to be bound by them, and as it has recently

We possess on this subject two texts, one of Pomponius and the other of Gaius(*a*). The first of these shews, very plainly, that what he is dealing with are the practical legal opinions, such as the jurisconsults of the Republic also used to give, and call by the same name. In old times, he says, they used to be delivered by anybody who chose, either orally, or in the form of a letter addressed to the judge. But Augustus desired to give an official character to this institution. He gave the *jus publice respondendi* to certain jurisconsults, who, in consequence, had power to respond *ex auctoritate ejus*, and whose responses, as the contrast made by Pomponius with the previous régime shews, had to be written and sealed, possibly to prevent falsifications, possibly to carry with them the indication of their source(*b*). And Pom-

been shewn sealed by him with a seal intended like our modern signature, to make them binding on him. See on the first point, · *Textes*, p. 803, and upon the second, *Textes*, pp. 820-822.

(*a*) Pomponius, *D.* 1, 2, *De o. j.*, 2, 48, 49; Gaius, 1, 7. Justinian, *Inst.*, 1, 2, *De j. nat.*, 8, merely reproduces and paraphrases the text of Gaius, and consequently has not the value of a third independent source.

(*b*) Usually the seal placed upon the *responsa prudentium* is understood as having the object of preventing the letter being opened before it reached its destination. But, since Zangemeister discovered among the vouchers of Pompeii seals placed not upon the straps which fastened the document to insure its being kept closed, but at the foot of the deed to certify the source from which it emanated (p. 141, n. z), we may ask, as Erman does, *Z. S. St.*, 20, 1899, p. 186, whether the seal of the jurisconsults may not have rather fulfilled the second function.

ponius adds that the practice begun by Augustus was continued by the succeeding emperors.

This innovation cannot have deprived the independent jurisconsults of the right to give legal opinions. Labeo, for example, was very active in giving opinions, although there is nothing to indicate that he had the *jus publice respondendi*. But it gave to the opinions of the certificated jurisconsults a special authority, which they are sometimes said to have had at first *de facto* only, but which must rather have been *de jure*, (as was later that of the rescripts), and have controlled the judge in respect to the trial in view whereof the opinion had been given, conditionally on the facts having been accurately stated.

This is attested by Gaius in the second of the texts, by the fact that he excepts only the case where there were several discordant responses in reference to the same trial, in which case a rescript of Hadrian said that the judge remained free. In point of fact, Hadrian's rescript is often looked upon as having introduced a new right; but it may quite as probably, and even more so, have been confirmatory of a pre-existing condition of things.

However, the same text of Gaius has brought a much graver complication into the question by apparently attributing to the *responsa* obligatory force, not only in the specific trials for which they had been obtained, but in all others, and to the opinions of the certified jurisconsults, not only when given after consultation, but universally. He interprets *responsa* by *sententiae et opiniones eorum qui permissionem habent jura condendi*, and he says these *responsa* had the force of law if they were in agreement. On the strength of that, many authorities have conceded the conclusion that, at any rate after Hadrian's rescript, legislative force must have attached, at all the trials in which they were invoked, to all the opinions of the certified jurisconsults, whether living or dead. But this admission would imply a system astonishingly complicated in practice, and still more astonishingly inconsistent with the jealous nature of the imperial power. The great probability is, that in spite of his peculiar and perhaps corrupted formula, Gaius means to speak exclusively, as Pomponius does, of *responsa* invoked in the trial of the case for which they had been given. As to the writings of the jurisconsults, legislative force was not accorded to them until long after the death of their authors, by the law of the succeeding period.

Section II.—The Absolute Monarchy(a).

I.—Organisation of public powers(b).

From the beginning of the period which runs from the accession of Diocletian (A.D. 284) to the death of Justinian (A.D. 565), the more or less efficacious limitations of the imperial authority which have suggested the term 'diarchy' in reference to the principate, definitely disappeared. The new system, the main features of which were traced by Diocletian, and which was almost completed under Constantine, left subsisting, out of the three powers which had been for centuries the theoretical foundation of the State, only the magistracy, or, more

(a) This introduction being primarily a sketch of political institutions, I have not hesitated to draw a line between the two periods of the Empire at Diocletian's reform. From the point of view of the history of private law, properly so called, the line of demarcation would seem to be afforded by Constantine, with whom, in the first place, Christianity came into power, the influence of which, though often exaggerated, nevertheless does clearly shew itself in certain directions, and principally in the laws relating to second marriages, to divorce and to legitimisation—and, with whom especially, in the second place, from a wider and more definite juridical point of view, there begins a new legislative phase, very barbaric but quite prolific, marked at the same time by a most conspicuous decadence in point of technique, and by an audacity often surprising. See on the law-making activity of Constantine, the information furnished by Mitteis, *Reichsrecht und Volksrecht*, 1891, p. 548 *et seq.*

(b) Bruns-Lenel, *Gesch. und Quell.*, §§ 57-62. Mommsen, *Abriss*, pp. 347-363.

accurately, only the imperial authority. By a new system of succession to the throne, the people were robbed of the formal power of instituting the new emperor. The senate was transformed into a sort of municipal assembly of the city of Rome, along with which soon came into existence another senate—equal in authority and, moreover, similarly municipal—at Constantinople. As to the magistrates,—that is to say, the old Republican magistrates,—it was the consuls alone who retained any importance; they continued to give the date to the year, and were consequently appointed by the emperor. The others continued to exist, but with functions of a merely municipal character, such as the prætors and the quæstors; or else only in name, as in the case of the tribunes.

The sole authority from which all flowed, by way of a firmly established hierarchy, was the imperial authority, which, moreover, assumed at that period a somewhat strange aspect by reason of the division of the Empire into two parts, the East and the West,—each governed by an Augustus, who had at his side, as an auxiliary and heir presumptive, a Cæsar; and each with its separate administration, (i.e., government, finances, and army); while legislation was common. It is not incumbent on us here to study the successive phases of this dualism, which at first was not permanent, but only became so after Valentinian I. Neither is it necessary to give many details about the division of different public offices (all of which were conferred by the emperor and paid by salary) between central and local, civil and military administration. Conformably to the system of absolute monarchy, and perhaps in imitation of that of the Persians, the central administration characteristically mingled together genuinely political officers, the ministers, with personages fulfilling purely domestic functions near the person of the Prince; and placed the *praepositus sacri cubiculi*, who was chamberlain, side by side with the chancellor of the Empire, with the *quaestor sacri palatii*. In inferior grades, military authority was thereafter rigorously separated from civil authority. As to civil administration, for the purpose of which justice, finance, and administration properly so called were united in the same hands, the administrative unit—made separate from the areas of military jurisdictions, so as to prevent concert between the authorities of the two orders,—was the province, much smaller than the old provinces, and managed by a governor, called according to his rank *consularis, praeses, rector,* or by some such title. Several provinces formed a diocese, *dioecesis,* subject to a *vicarius;* lastly, the *dioeceses* were joined together into prefectures under the governance of the prefects of the *praetorium,* the number of which at one time, (though perhaps without the system ever having been definitely fixed), was four :—The Orient, Illyria, Italy and Gaul(c).

(o) This hierarchy referred to in the text is principally known to us through a list of the officers of the Empire, accompanied with information as to their insignia, troops, and subordinates, the *notitia dignitatum,* evidently taken from the official almanac of the Empire kept duly entered up at the seat of the central power,

II.—The law and the original authorities.

The legislation(d) was, generally speaking, in all cases common to the two parts of the Empire which considered themselves as two fractions of one and the same whole; and it was only at a late date, and on rare occasions, that the law made for the one part was refused recognition in the other part. But there was remaining only one source of law which had not become exhausted(e), which continued to produce new law, side by side with the law already created in the past. This was, as the logic of the system demanded, the imperial constitutions, the expression of the Master's will, which, as late as Diocletian, continued to be drawn up in an excellent juridical style, but from the time of Constantine, on the contrary, were written in execrable language, both inappropriate and diffuse, and which, nevertheless, were the principal factors in that transformation of the classi-

---

and covering the period between A.D. 411 and A.D. 413. The latest edition is that of Seeck, 1876; the older one of Boecking, 1839-1856, is still valuable on account of its commentary.

(d) Krueger, *Sources*, §§ 32-33. Bruns-Lenel, *Gesch. und Quell.*, § 66.

(e) Custom itself was deprived by Constantine, C., 8, 52 (53), *Quae sit longa consuet.*, 2, of the power *vincere rationem aut legem*, which means, as it would seem, of the power to abrogate existing law. On the proposed methods of harmonizing this text and the fragment of Julianus acknowledging its functions and reproduced likewise by Justinian (p. 106, n. cc), see, for example, besides Pernice's article there referred to, Regelsberger, *Pandekten*, p. 103.

cal law which was recorded, rather than accomplished, by Justinian.

These constitutions now comprehended but few *mandata*. On the other hand, the Byzantine emperors issued many rescripts almost indistinguishable from decrees by reason of the development of the procedure *per rescriptum* (pp. 125-6). But for this very reason, these rescripts came to have in principle no authority except for the cases in which they were issued,—a fact which naturally led to their posting up being discontinued. The emperor principally exercised his law-making power in the form of *edicta*, of *leges edictales*, addressed either to the senate, like the old orationes *in senatu habitae*, or to the people, or to magistrates, especially to the prefects of the *praetorium*.

The imperial constitutions being the sole active source of law, the only modification affecting the positive authority of the law derived from the ancient sources naturally emanated from them. That law was always in operation in its integrity. But, instead of reverting to the original texts of the laws,—the *senatusconsulta*, or the edicts, for example,—it was customary to take as texts the works of the commentators, following a practice which, according to some modern authorities, dated, by virtue of the *permissio jura condendi*, from ·Hadrian or even Augustus (p. 146), but which, in reality, was unknown at that time, and must have developed itself normally, in proportion as the value of living jurisconsults diminished, and admiration for the jurisconsults of the past increased. This practice was bound necessarily to bring with it abuses, to induce astute men of law to attempt the deception of poorly instructed *judices* by bewildering them with specious citations from ancient jurisconsults. Ammianus Marcelinus cites, in the fourth century, some advocates of his own time, whose citations were habitually confined to Trebatius and Cascellius, and who undertook to find texts (*lectiones pollicentur*), to justify all iniquities, even the murder of a mother by her son(*f*).

The imperial authority intervened, on two occasions, by constitutions intended to rob this practice of its disadvantages, at the same time that they legalised it. A constitution of Constantine of A.D. 321 decreed the abolition of the notes of Paulus and of Ulpian on Papinian, so as to make the authority of the last prevail, and at the same time confirmed the authority of the Sentences of Paulus(*g*). Then, a century later, a reform infinitely more fundamental was attempted, in A.D. 426, by the Law of Citations of Theodosius II and Valentinian III(*h*). This legislative enactment, which is well known, but some details of which are obscure, established between the writings of the jurisconsults the system of majority of votes, while, in case of disagreement, giving

(*f*) Ammianus Marcelinus, 30, 4, 11 *et seq.*, and Pernice, *Gesch. und Quell.*, p. 165.

(*g*) C. Th., 9, 43, *De sent. pass.*, 1. Cf. C. Th., 1, 4, *De resp. prud.*, 1, 2.

(*h*) C. Th., 1, 4, *De resp. prud.*, 3.

the preponderance to Papinian, and again excluding the notes written on his works by Ulpian and Paulus. But what jurisconsults might figure in this calculation? It is often said that the only ones who could be cited, were Papinian, Paulus, Ulpian, Modestinus, and Gaius (who now for the first time figures among the *juris auctores*). Nevertheless this is not quite what the constitution says. It selects as proper for citation the five jurisconsults and the authors cited by them, which would comprehend nearly all the authors, notably Q. Mucius Scaevola, Sabinus, Julianus, and Marcellus,—but only subject to this reservation, that these might not be cited excepting on the condition of confirming the citation by producing the original work. The result was no doubt practically that one could cite only the five. But this did not prevent the writings of the others from always having the same authority in point of law.

These works, together with certain ancient monuments of the law, collectively constituted at this period, what is called the *jus*, in opposition to the constitutions, which are called the *leges*(*i*) ; and it is on the basis of this division that Justinian made the compilations which have handed down to us the largest number of documents of both kinds. But the work of compilation neither commenced with him, nor ended with him. I shall, therefore, rapidly enumerate here the different compilations of the later law, first taking those of the *jus* and *leges*, either

(*i*) See Krueger, p. 347, n. 1, with the references.

separately or together, which were made before his time, then his compilations, and lastly, the principal later collections.

1. **Collections prior to Justinian.**—There had been before Justinian, in the case of *leges*, three special collections, two private and one official, all three bearing the novel ·name of *codex*, which probably was derived from the fact that instead of being written on rolls of papyrus, the earliest ones had been made of separate leaves fastened together like the tablets of the *codices* (p. 143, note), and like the sheets of parchment of manuscripts(*j*).

The two private collections are the Gregorian and Hermogenian Codes, the second being a completion of the first. The former of these was made about A.D. 294 by some one named Gregorius, probably a professor at the school of Berytus(*k*); and the latter between A.D. 314 and A.D. 324 by some one named Hermogenianus, as to whom it is not known whether he is the jurisconsult of the Digest or not (p. 136). The names of the two compilers, for long a matter of dispute, have been determined with certainty by inference from the forms of names in use at that time(*l*).

These two codes contain the imperial constitutions:—the former (which was divided into books and into titles), those from Hadrian to A.D. 294, and the latter (which

---

(*j*) Th. Mommsen, *Z. S. St.*, 10, 1889, p. 345 *et seq*.
(*k*) Th. Mommsen, *Z. S. St.*, 22, 1901, pp. 139-144.
(*l*) Th. Mommsen, *Z. S. St.*, 10, 1889, p. 347 *et seq*.

consisted of a single book divided into titles), those from
the year 294 to the year 324, and even, by virtue of successive additions, to the year 365. It is from the first
that all the constitutions of Justinian's Code which date
before the time of Constantine (p. 163) are taken, though
that Code also probably contains a certain number coming from the second. But the remains of them which
have come down to us directly are not numerous(*m*).

We have many more remains of the official collection,
the Theodosian code, a collection of imperial constitutions subsequent to Constantine, and promulgated in
A.D. 438, by Theodosius II in the East, and Valentinian
III in the West. It is composed of sixteen books divided
into titles, in which the constitutions are placed in their
chronological order. As to arrangement, it follows, on
the whole, the order of the *digesta* (p. 137). After the
sources comes the *pars edictalis* (books 2 to 4) ; then the
second part, with the new complementary matters (books
5 to 15), and a sixteenth book devoted to the law of the
Church. It was supplanted in the East by the legislation
of Justinian, so that all the remains of it which have
come down to us come from the West. These consist of
certain manuscripts containing parts of the original
work, and the manuscripts of the *Lex Romana* of the
Visigoths (p. 158), which contains an abridgement of it.

(*m*) Ed. Haenel, 1837. The best text to refer to now is that
given in a somewhat fragmentary form, but more complete and
more accurate, by Krueger, *Coll. lib. juris*, 3. See Krueger,
Sources, § 34.

Even when put together, they leave some gaps which unfortunately occur principally in the part relating to the private law(*n*). With it are always cited the post-Theodosian novels, being constitutions issued in the two Empires down to the fall of the Western Empire in 476(*nn*).

Along with these collections of *leges*, we find, in the period prior to Justinian, certain official and private compilations embracing at the same time the *jus* and the *leges*.

Among the private compilations, the most important are: (1) The *fragmenta Vaticana*, a palimpsest manu-

---

(*n*) Cf. Krueger, *Sources*, § 35. The last complete edition, produced by Haenel in 1842, was not perfectly satisfactory as regards establishment of the correct text, and was not altogether up to date (cf. *Codicis Theodosiani fragmenta Taurinensia*, ed. P. Krueger, 1880). The old edition of Jacques Godefroy (ed. Ritter, 1736-1745, 7 vols. folio) is even more imperfect, and incomplete, as to the text, but still remains very important by reason of the commentary. An edition displaying much learning and provided with an *apparatus criticus* of the highest excellence, and to the preparation of which the illustrious Mommsen, who died in November, 1903, had devoted the last years of his life, has just been published (*Theodosiani libri XVI cum constitutionibus Sirmondianis et leges novellae ad Theodosianum pertinentes ediderunt Th. Mommsen et Paulus M. Meyer. Vol. I., Theodosiani libri XVI cum constitutionibus Sirmondianis edidit* Th. Mommsen, Berlin, 1905).

(*nn*) Ed. Haenel, 1844. A new edition of it will be brought out by Paul M. Meyer in the second volume (at present in the press) of the edition of the Theodosian code mentioned in the preceding note.

script, discovered in 1820, in the Vatican, by Cardinal Angelo Mai, which contains the fragments of a systematic work of the fourth century relating both to *jus* and to *leges*, and is valuable because it reproduces some of the more ancient texts without modification(*o*); (2) The *collatio legum Mosaicarum et Romanarum*, a long fragment of the first book of a work in which a Christian author of the end of the fourth century, or the beginning of the fifth century, brings together passages of laws attributed to Moses and texts of Roman law taken from the jurisconsults of the Law of Citations and from the first two codes,—with what object it is not known, unless it was to shew the want of originality of the Roman law, whose precepts are found already existing in the law of Moses(*p*); (3) The Syro-Roman book, an incomplete and imperfect exposition of Roman law made in the East, about the year 476 (probably for the use of ecclesiastical tribunals, where it had not been supplanted by Justinian's compilations), and originally written in Greek, and then translated into Syriac, whence this translation afterwards passed into Armenian and into Arabic, to come down to us in the Syriac, Arabic, and Armenian texts(*q*).

(*o*) *Textes*, p. 435.

(*p*) *Textes*, p. 496. See also the notices relating to the Sinaitic fragments, p. 578, and to the *consultatio*, p. 590. Max Conrat, Hermes, 1900, pp. 344-347, has ventured the suggestion that the unknown author of the *collatio* may be St. Jerome.

(*q*) A learned edition of it was published by Bruns and Sachau, *Syrischrömisches Rechtsbuch aus dem fünften Jahrun-*

The official compilations are those made of the Roman
law applicable in their States by order of the kings of the
barbarian invaders(r). The most interesting for us is
the *Lex Romana* of the Visigoths, a compilation of the
jus and the *leges* made in the year 506 by order of Alaric
II for his Roman subjects. This compilation,—which does
not bear any official title in the manuscripts, and which
our authors of the sixteenth century designate by the
name of the *breviarium Alarici*, but which is generally
called nowadays the *lex Romana Visigothorum,*—gives as
leges extracts from the Theodosian code and the post-
Theodosian novels, as *jus* the abridgment in two books
of the Institutes of Gaius, the extracts already mentioned
from the Sentences of Paulus, extracts from the Gregorian and Hermogenian codes (classed therefore in the
jus), and as a closing extract, a fragment of Papinian,
placed there as a mark of honour. The different texts,
except the Epitome of Gaius, are accompanied by an
Interpretatio, which at one time was believed also to be
the work of Alaric's commissioners, but which is generally thought nowadays to have been composed like the
Epitome itself, at a prior date in the course of the fifth
century, and which constitutes a document of value for

---

derte, 1880; and two excellent analyses have been produced
by Brinz, *K. V. J.,* 1880, p. 548 *et seq.,* and Esmein, *Mélanges,* p.
403 *et seq.*

(r) Bruns-Lenel, §§ 73-74; Brunner, *Deutsche Rechtsges-*
chichte, 1, 1887, §§ 48-53; Esmein, *Hist. du droit français,* p.
109 *et seq.;* Krueger, *Sources,* § 41; Brissaud, *Manuel d'histoire*
du droit, p. 67 *et seq.*

the knowledge of the Roman law of that time. Notwithstanding the rapid fall of the domination of the Visigoths in the Gauls, the collection remained much in vogue in Southern France during the Middle Ages, and a large number of manuscripts of it have come down to us, some of them abridgements, some of them complete and even supplemented by additions and corrections derived from pure Roman sources(s).

Besides this, the *Lex Romana Burgundionum* must be mentioned, drawn up, in accordance with an engagement entered into by Gondebaud when he caused the barbarian law of the Burgundians to be compiled. He had promised to do the same thing for the law of his Roman subjects, and the promise was kept probably before his death in 516,—certainly before the fall of the kingdom of the Burgundians in 534. The titles of this *Lex,* —relating to penal law, private law, and procedure,—follow the order of the Barbarian law. The sources, only . indicated in exceptional cases, are the three codes, the Sentences of Paulus, a work of Gaius (his Institutes or his *Regulae*), and the *Interpretationes.* After the Frankish conquest, it was utilised to complete the Breviary, and is often found following that in the manuscripts; whence the error, found as early as in the manuscripts

(s) Ed. Haenel, 1849, The text of a palimpsest manuscript subsequently discovered is contained in *Legis Romanae Visigothorum fragmenta ex cod. palimps. S. Legion. eccl.,* Madrid, 1896. A dogmatic statement of the law contained in this compilation is given in Max Conrat, *Breviarium Alaricianum, römisches Recht im fränkischen Reich,* 1903.

of the ninth century, by which its title is taken from the name of the author of the last fragment of the Breviary, *Papinianus,* abridges to *Papianus* (*t*).

The edict of Theodoric,—issued by Theodoric, king of the Ostrogoths, probably at the beginning of the sixth century, certainly after the year 493, and which summarises in 155 articles a law applicable both to the Goths and the Romans,—contains no indication of sources or even of textual citations. It is only by comparison that we see that its authors have derived material at any rate from the three codes, the Sentences of Paulus, and the *Interpretationes.* Consequently, it has less interest for the Roman law than the Roman law has for it (*u*). The same is true in a still greater degree of other barbarian laws, such as the *Lex Romana Raetica Curiensis* (*v*); which is a sufficient reason for saying nothing further about them here.

II.—Justinian's Compilations. The emperor Justinian, who was called to the throne in 527 by his uncle Justin, and who died in 565, owes a unique celebrity in

(*t*) Ed. in the *Monumenta Germaniae*, by Bluhme, *Leges, III.*, 1863, p. 579 *et seq.*, and by De Salis, *Legum sectio* 1, 4to, 2; 1892, pp. 3-188. The old edition by Barkow, *Lex Romana Burgundionum*, 1826, contains a commentary which is still useful.

(*u*) Ed. Bluhme, 1870, *Monumenta Germaniae, Leges, V.*, p. 146 *et seq.* Cf. Gaudenzi, *Gli editti di Theodorico*, 1884, and *Z. S. St.*, *Germ. Abth.*, 7, 1886, pp. 29-52.

(*v*) Ed. Zeumer *Monumenta Germaniae, Leges, V.*, 1889, pp. 289-542. Cf. the same *Z. S. St.*, *Germ. Abth.*, 9, 1888, pp. 8-52.

the history of Roman law(*w*), to the juridical compilations made in his reign and by his order, probably at the suggestion of his favourite, Tribonian(*x*).

The work was begun as early as A.D. 528, with the *leges*. A commission was charged, on February 15th of this year, to combine in a single collection the constitutions in force, by revising the three former codes, by adding later constitutions which had not been abrogated, and by suppressing repetitions and contradictions. The work was finished in 529, and the Code published on April 7th, to take the effect of law from the 16th.

For the *jus*, the task was a little more difficult. Apparently there was an unwillingness to undertake the enterprise before the adoption of a certain number of authoritative decisions making a clean sweep of what was

(*w*) It is quite unnecessary to concern ourselves here with the political history or with the biography of Justinian, for which the principal source, of very questionable value, as we know, is the Secret History of Procopius. Mr. James Bryce has demonstrated (*English Historical Review*, 1887, pp. 657-686) the apocryphal character of the pretended life of Justinian by the Abbot Theophilus from which come many of the details of the current biography of Justinian. Cf. Krumbacher, *Byzantinische Litteraturgeschichte* (Iwan Müller, *Handbuch*, 9, 1), 2nd ed., 1897, p. 237.

(*x*) See on the history and the different elements of Justinian's codification, Bruns-Lenel, *Gesch. und Quell.*, § 70; Krueger, *Sources*, §§ 42-48, 52-53. Some details and a more complete bibliography will be found in my two articles in the *Grande Encyclopedie* ' *Digeste de Justinien* ' and ' *Institutes de Justinien.*'

antiquated, which were issued in A.D. 529, 530, and 531, and of which a collection seems to have been made under the name of the *Quinquaginta Decisiones*. It was only on December 15th, A.D. 530, that Justinian issued a constitution instructing Tribonian, the *quaestor sacri palatii*, to form a commission charged with the collection of extracts from the jurisconsults, which should be for the *jus* what the Code was for the *leges*. The commission, formed of professors and practitioners, carried on their work with great rapidity, and it reached its completion at the end of the year 532, by the official recognition of a collection designated by the Latin and Greek names of *Digesta* or Πανδεκται, and promulgated on December 16th, A.D. 533, to come into force on December 30th. Justinian had furthermore caused to be drawn up in the interval a manual inspired by Gaius, and bearing, as his did, the name of *Institutiones*, which was promulgated some days previously, on November 21st, A.D. 533, to have likewise the force of law from December 30th. On the other hand, no longer judging the first edition of the Code in harmony with the innovations made by him since the year 529, he published in 534, under the name of the *Codex Repetitae Praelectionis*, a revised edition of it, which supplanted the first, and which alone has come down to us. Lastly, he subsequently issued a certain number of other constitutions, for the most part in the Greek language, of which no official collections were made, and which are called the 'Novels' (*novellae constitutiones*, νεαραί διατάξεις). —To sum up, leaving out of account the first edition of the Code, and the *Quinquaginta Decisiones,* which have not come down to us, there were four principal component parts: Institutes, Digest, Code, and Novels.

The Code (*codex Justinianus, codex repelitae praelectionis*) was drawn up on the plan of the former codes, which was that of the *digesta* of the jurisconsults (p. 137), with a preamble on the sources and the magistracies. It consists of twelve books divided into titles, each under a rubric. Under each title the constitutions or laws, which run from the time of Hadrian to A.D. 534, are reproduced in chronological order, but with many suppressions and amendments (*interpolationes, emblemata Triboniani*) intended to bring them into accord with the law in force. These interpolations have, up to the present, been less studied in the Code than in the Digest, but those in the former are neither more doubtful nor less interesting for the period from Hadrian down to and comprising Diocletian(*y*). The very complicated history of the transmission of the text of the Code may be divided into two phases:—a phase of concentration, when everything that appeared superfluous in the manuscripts was suppressed, *i.e.,* the three last books relating to penal and administrative law, the

(*y*) See some examples in Gradenwitz, *Bull. dell'ist. di d. R.,* 2, 1889, pp. 3-15. Cf. also the studies of H. Krueger upon the language of the constitutions of the Code, Woelflin's *Archiv,* X., pp. 247-252, XI., pp. 453-467, and the vocabulary of the Latin constitutions of Justinian by Longo, *Bull. dell'ist. di d. R.,* 10, 1897-1898.

constitutions in the Greek language, and, in the case of the constitutions retained, the superscription, placed at their head, and indicating their authors and those to whom they were addressed, and their subscriptions, placed at the end, giving their date and their place of issue; then a phase of reintegration, when people laboriously restored, either by the help of fragments of the ancient manuscripts or by the help of Greek sources, what had been previously destroyed. The best modern edition of it has been produced by Krueger(z).

The Digest (*Digesta Justiniana*) is divided into fifty books, all of them subdivided into several titles, except books 30-32. The titles, furnished with rubrics, are divided into statements of law or fragments. These are extracts from jurisconsults, adapted to the law in force at the date of the completion of the collection, whence arises the necessity of searching out interpolations and suppressions, which have, up to the present, been much more studied in their case, than in the case of the constitutions of the Code(a). Lastly, these fragments

(z) *Codex Justinianus, recognovit P. Krueger*, 1877. The text and the most important notes are reproduced in the stereotype edition which forms volume II of the *Corpus Juris Civilis* of Mommsen, Krueger and Schoell.

(a) The interpolations which have placed in the texts the law of Justinian's time in place of that of the time of the codified jurisconsults, are discovered by three different processes, sometimes demanding very delicate handling. Interpolation to begin with, reveals itself in concrete fashion when two discordant versions of the same text are found in an original source and in the

—which indicate their source by name of author, work, and (if there be occasion) book, and which nowadays are numbered,—are also subdivided, when of any consider-

compilation (*F. V.*, 12, and *D.*, 18, 6, *De per. et comm.* 19, 1; Gaius, 3, 140. 143, and *D.* 19, 2, *Locati*, 25 pr.). But it may be established with equal certainty when the same text has been given in two places by the compilers (*leges geminatae*) and they have amended it only in one of the two (*D.*, 1, 10, *De off. cons.*, 1, 2, and 40, 2, *De manum vind.*, 20, 4). Again it may manifest itself in peculiarities of style, in hellenisms, in the employment of words and idioms of low latin unknown to the jurisconsults and familiar to Justinian, and sometimes, also, in breaks in grammatical continuity, which arise from pure negligence, *e. g.*, accusatives which are governed by nothing (*D.*, 39, 5, *De don.*, 28), pronouns in the feminine representing a masculine substantive (*De pign. act.*, 8, 3). It results logically from the interruption in the order of the ideas of the jurisconsults, and juridically from the impossibility of the jurisconsult having used the language which is attributed to him. Lastly, it may be rendered probable in the case of some groups of texts, by the way in which the jurisconsult treats the matter dealt with in the correlative part of the work cited, as has been demonstrated by Lenel, with great success, in the case of commentaries on the edict, and the works which follow the same arrangement (the transferring to usucapion of the explanations given about *accessio possessionum* in the interdict *utrubi*, to the *actio ex stipulatu duplae* of the rules of the *actio auctoritatis*, to the *actio empti* of those of the *actio de modo agri*, to the *actio pigneraticia* of those of the *actio fiduciae*, to the *pactum constituti* of those of the *receptum argentarii*, &c). Practically, the *Palingenesia* of the same Lenel points out many interpolated texts. I shall only mention in connection with this line of studies, taken up again with much zeal during late years, the special works of Gradenwitz (*Interpolationen in den Pandekten*, 1887. *Z. S. St.* 6, 1885, p. 56 *et seq.*; 7, 1, 1886, p. 45 *et seq.*; *Bull dell'ist.*, 1889, p. 3

able length, into *principium* and paragraphs. The general arrangement of the titles is, with some systematic modifications, that of the Code, and consequently that of the *Digesta*. As to that of the fragments in the titles, it remained undetected up to our century, when Bluhme discovered, in 1818, the method according to which the commissioners who originated it proceeded in their work(*b*). The works to be extracted were divided into three groups, or three collections, leading off, in the case of the first, with the *libri ad Sabinum*, of the second, with the *libri ad edictum*, and of the third, with the

et *seq.*) and of Eisele (*Z. S. St.*, 7, 1, 1886, p. 16 *et seq.*; 10, 1889, p. 296 *et seq.*; 11, 1890, p. 1 *et scq.*; 13, 1892, p. 118 *et seq.*; 18, 1897, p. 1 *et seq.*), and in an inverse sense, on the possibility of establishing by a counter-examination based on the language of Justinian, the purity of texts suspected of interpolations, the observations of Kalb, *Die Jagd nach Interpolationen in den Digesten*, 1897. We may reasonably expect a new harvest of results from the researches, similarly resumeu very actively in late years, into the language of the jurisconsults and juridical latinity. See Kalb, *Das Juristenlatein*, 2nd ed., 1888, and *Roms Juristen nach ihrer Sprache dargestellt*, 1890, and especially the *Vocabularium Jurisprudentiae Romanae* taken in hand by O. Gradenwitz, B. Kuebler and E. Th. Schulze, and continued by B. Kuebler and R. Helm (vol. I., A.-C., 1894,—A 1903). When this work is completed, it will render superfluous the far from satisfactory dictionaries of juridical latinity on which we have to rely at present.

(*b*) Cf., however, the adverse contention of F. Hoffmann, *Die Compilation der Digesten Justinians*, 1900. But see the decisive answers made in *Z. S. St.*, 22, 1901, by Mommsen, pp. 1-11, and P. Krueger, pp. 12-49, and in the *Realencylopädie* of Pauly-Wissowa, see *Digesta*, pp. 520-541, by Jörs.

works of Papinian (Sabinian series, Edictal series, Papinian series.) Each of these collections was entrusted to a sub-commission, and then the extracts made by each sub-commission were placed one after the other in each title, in a variable order, however, and with frequent interchanges, and sometimes, also, with the addition of texts from a fourth collection, possibly made as an afterthought(c). As to the manuscripts, the long-disputed problem of their respective value appears to have been definitely settled by Mommsen. The only ancient manuscript is,—with some small palimpsest fragments which are at Naples, and some sheets of papyrus, which are at Pommersfelden,—an excellent manuscript written by Greek copyists in the sixth or seventh century, and called the Florentine, because it has been, since 1406, at Florence, or the *littera Pisana*, because it was previously at Pisa. It is true there exists a very large number of manuscripts of the eleventh and twelfth centuries containing a text of the Digest (usually divided into three parts: *digestum vetus, infortiatum,* and *digestum novum*), which is generally called, to distinguish it, *littera vulgaris* or *Vulgate*. But Mommsen has proved that the manuscripts of the Vulgate are all derived from a single manuscript, which was copied from the Floren-

(c) Mommsen's great edition of the Digest indicates, in the case of each text, to what collection it belongs, and the same references are collected together, in the stereotype edition, at the beginning of each title. And at the end of both will be found a table of the distribution of works between the four collections.

tine, but collated with an independent manuscript, now lost, furnishing some valuable corrections as far as book 35. It is on the basis of this principle that he has established the text of his edition of the Digest, which is to-day incomparably the best(d).

The Institutes of Justinian (*Justiniani Institutiones*) are a manual in four books, divided into titles provided with rubrics, and nowadays into paragraphs, written on the plan of the Institutes of Gaius. They are composed, like the Digest, almost exclusively of extracts from jurisconsults, but without any indication of source; and they have been taken sometimes from the Digest, but oftener from original works of the same class(e). The drawing of them up was entrusted to a commission of three members, Tribonian, Dorotheus, and Theophilus, amongst whom, as has been shewn by philological reasoning, the work was equally divided into two halves (probably between Theophilus and Dorotheus), while Tribonian reserved for himself the presidency. The Insti-

---

(d) *Digesta Justiniani Augusti recognovit Th. Mommsen*, 2 vols., Berlin, 1866-1870. The text and the most important notes are reproduced in the stereotype edition, which is found in volume I of the *Corpus* of Mommsen, Krueger and Schoell. The history of the manuscripts is set forth in the preface of the large edition. A phototypic reproduction of the Florentine manuscript has been undertaken in Italy.

(e) See upon this point Ferrini, *Rendiconti dell'ist. Lombardo*, 23, 1890, pp. 131-180; *Bull. dell'ist di D. R.*, 13, 1900, pp. 101-207; Appleton, *R. gén. de droit*, 1890, pp. 12-41, 97-125. In a contrary sense, Mispoulet, *N. R. hist.*, 1890, pp. 5-30.

tutes have been transmitted to us by somewhat defective manuscripts, of which none go further back than the ninth century. The best modern edition is that of Krueger(f).

As to the Novels, three private collections of them have come down to us:—two Latin ones, the *Epitome* of Julianus, and the *Authenticum,* and one Greek one, the most complete, known to the Western world only since the fifteenth century. The best modern edition, begun by Schoell and concluded after his death by Kroll(g), gives both the text of the Greek collection, accompanied by a Latin translation, and the Latin text of the *Authenticum.*

Such are the four component parts, which, for some centuries, it· has been customary to unite, with some additions, under the name of the *Corpus juris,* or,—by way of contrast to the *Corpus juris canonici,*—of the *Corpus juris civilis.* These constitute for us Justinian's work, a work very important in itself, and still more important through the influence which it has exercised upon the science and the practice of the law. This work has sometimes been over-praised, and sometimes over-depreciated. Without speaking of other less essential points, Justin-

(f) First in 1867, in a first edition octavo; then, with some corrections in volume I of the stereotype edition of the *Corpus,* then, in 1899, in a second edition octavo (Berlin, Weidmann). This is the text of the *Corpus* which I have usually followed in the edition of the Institutes contained in my *Textes,* p. 560 *et seq.*

(g) *Corpus juris civilis, ed. stereotypa,* III: *Novellae, recognovit R. Schoell opus absolvit G. Kroll,* 1870-1895.

ian has been justly reproached with having, in his work of codification, perpetuated the purely historical separation of *jus* and *leges*, and with having, save in the Novels, proceeded by way of cutting and clipping, instead of himself writing his own laws. But these two legislative imperfections have proved to possess for us two advantages which he did not foresee; for they enable us the better to discover, between the lines of his compilations, that anterior law, the history of which we are so desirous of learning, and for the study of which they still constitute the most extensive collection of materials.

3. **Works posterior to Justinian**(*h*).—Justinian had the fatuity to forbid as useless and mischievous all commentaries, in any proper sense of the term, which any one might desire to make on his compilations But if this prohibition had an influence on the form of later legal works, it did not prevent his codification from being, as is generally the case, the point of departure of a mass of literature which commenced before his death, and only ended with the fall of the Eastern empire. Of this literature, I shall merely mention, as being the most indispensable monuments for the knowledge of the law of Justinian, and of the former law: (1) The Greek paraphrase of the Institutes, which is generally attributed to Justinian's collaborator, Theophilus, and seems to have been composed very shortly after their

(*h*) Krueger, *Sources*, §§ 49-50. Bruns-Lenel, *Gesch. und Quell.*, § 72.

publication, and before the appearance of the second edition of the Code. It contains, in the midst of many surprising errors, some useful information, notably upon the law anterior to Justinian(*i*). (2) The *Basilica*, a Greek compilation, divided into sixty books, and subdivided into titles, of all the law of Justinian still in force in the ninth century, in which each title brings into synthesis the corresponding texts of the Institutes, the Digest, the Code, and the Novels, and which was afterwards completed by an apparatus of *Scholia* drawn from the whole of the Greek juridical literature. The *Basilica* were drawn up by order of Leo the Philosopher. (888-911), and the *Scholia* were added to them in the course of the tenth century. We possess the *Basilica* almost complete, and the *Scholia* in great part(*j*). (3) In the West, the Turin gloss of the Institutes(*k*), (so-called from the manuscript of the Institutes on the

(*i*) New edition by Ferrini, *Institutionum Graeca paraphrasis Theophilo antecessori vulgo tributa,* 1884-1897. An older edition by Reitz, *Theophili antecessoris paraphrasis Graeca Institutionum,* 2 vols., 1754.

(*j*) The best edition, though defective, is that of Heimbach, *Basilicorum libri LX ed. E. Heimbach,* 7 vols., 1833-1897 (volume 7 is a supplement due to Ferrini and Mercati). The other most important Byzantine juridical works are to be found in Zachariae, *Jus Graeco-Romanum,* 7 vols., 1856-1884. See also, upon the history of the Byzantine law, Mortreuil, *Histoire du droit byzantin,* 3 vols., 1843; Zachariae, *Historia juris Graeco-Romani,* 1839, and *Geschichte des griechischrömischen Rechts,* 3rd edition, 1892 (*Histoire du droit privé gréco-romain,* translation of the first edition by Lauth, 1870).

(*k*) Ed. Krueger, *Z. R. G.,* 7, p. 44 *et seq.*

margin of which it is found), a collection of Latin *Scholia* on the Institutes, written in the time of Justinian, and the author of which seems to have had at his disposal some original sources now lost(*l*).

(*l*) In addition to the juridical monuments properly so-called, it is desirable, for the sake of completeness, to make some mention of the information furnished by legal documents, and lay authors. As to legal documents, in addition to what is cited by Krueger, *Sources*, § 39, there must be especially mentioned the rich collection of the papyri of Ravenna of the fifth, sixth, and seventh centuries, published with an excellent commentary by Gaetona Marini *Papiri diplomatici*, 1805) As to the literary sources, over and above the *scriptores historiae Augustae*, criticism of which should be taken up anew from the juridical point of view as well as from other points of view, on the basis of the works recently published on the subject of their true date, especially by Dessau, *Hermes*, 24, p. 337 *et seq.*, 27, p. 561 *et seq.*, and Mommsen, *Hermes*, 25, p. 228 *et seq.*, the following most certainly should be consulted: the letters of Symmacus, prefect of the City in A.D. 384 and 385, where there will be found some official letters to the Emperors which are of interest on the subjects of the procedure, and also the substance of the law; the commentaries of Bethmann-Hollweg, *Civilprozess*, 3, p. 352 *et seq.*, Kipp, *Litisdenuntiatio*, 1887, Baron, *Litisdenuntiatio*, 1887, and Ubbelohde, in Glück, series of books 43 and 44; edition O. Seeck, *Monumenta Germaniae*, 1883; the *Variae* of Cassiodorus, born in 482, died in 575, edited by Mommsen, *Monumenta Germaniae*, 1894, where there are some formularies of official acts (legitimation, *venia aetatis, &c.*); the letters of Sidonius Apollinaris, Bishop of Clermont, in the fifth century, of much interest in reference to the Roman law of the Barbarian epoch; cf. Esmein, *Mélanges*, p. 359 *et seq.*; editions of Baret, Paris, 1879, and Luthjohann, *Monumenta Germaniae*, 1887; the *Origines* of Isidorus of Seville, (died about 636,) which contains, especially in the fifth book, definitions of juridical terms borrowed from good sources. Bruns, *Fontes*, 2, pp. 82-86, gives the more important passages.

CHAPTER IV.

ROMAN LAW IN THE WEST.

It would be out of place to attempt here a real history of Roman law during the period which extends from the barbarian compilations and the collections of Justinian down to our own time. Nevertheless, perhaps the summary indication of a few salient points may serve as a useful guide across the wide space which separates the ancient texts from their modern interpreters.

Every one recognises nowadays that the transmission of Roman law has never been interrupted by a complete break in continuity, that in particular, even from an earlier date than the foundation of the school of Bologna, Roman law formed in France and Italy the subject of a system of instruction, and of a literature, which never entirely ceased. "Three points, however, may be discussed and are vigorously disputed:—the extent and the profundity of the instruction, the value of the scientific works, and the measure in which they were fitted, by reason of their method and contents, to serve as a model and a basis for the glossators"(m).

(m) Bruns-Lenel, *Gesch. und Quell.*, § 75; cf. Esmein, *Hist. du droit français*, p. 758 *et seq.;* Brissaud, *Manuel*, p. 170. The admirable work of Savigny, *Geschichte des römischen Rechts im Mittelalter*, 2nd ed., 1834-1851, remains always fundamental for

The work of the glossators(n) commenced at Bologna at the end of the eleventh century. Roman law had certainly been taught at Bologna before Irnerius, who began to be a professor there about 1088, and died after 1125. But from him dates the foundation of the celebrated school of jurisconsults which·bears the name of the "school of the glossators."

The glossators derive their name from the glosses, interlineal and marginal, by which they were in the habit of explaining the texts in the manuscripts, possibly following a usage borrowed from the ancient Lombard schools of law. But it is also necessary to mention among their works, the *casus*, in which they reconstituted the hypotheses upon which the texts proceed, and the *summae* in which they condensed, title by title, this or that compilation of Justinian. They have, by an exegetical labour of a very remarkable character,—and which still retains great value, notwithstanding glaring defects

the whole period which extends up to Alciati. But it has been found possible by later criticism to render the theories which he evolved more precise and correct, notably for the intermediate periods. The arguments in favour of the continuity have been particularly developed in the penetrating studies of Fitting. Cf., in a contrary sense, Flach, *Études critiques sur l'histoire du droit Romain au moyen âge*, Paris, 1890. The work, rich in information, of Max Conrat, *Geschichte der Quellen und Litteratur des römischen Rechts im früheren Mittelalter*, 1, 1889-1891, also accepts with some reserve the doctrines of Fitting.

(n) See, besides, volumes 3 to 5 of Savigny, Esmein, p. 761 . *et seq.*, and Brissaud, p. 192 *et seq.*, where the most recent literature will be found referred to.

arising from their ignorance of Roman history and literature,—ransacked minutely, both in their entirety and in detail, the texts of Justinian's compilations looked at as a body of law in active operation(o). The work of the glossators, (the most celebrated of whom after Irnerius, were Martinus, Bulgarus, Jacobus, and Hugo, called the four doctors, then Rogerius, then Placentinus, the professor of Montpellier, who died in 1192, and lastly, Otto and Azo), culminated, during the first third of the thirteenth century, with the publication of a methodical work of compilation, the Great Gloss, produced by Accursius (1182-1260), in which are to be found incorporated and classified the most important glosses of the different doctors, and which obtained an extraordinary success both as regards practice and theory.

The success of this compilation was, as often happens, the symptom of a decadence, which it only sufficed to accentuate in its turn. The Gloss became a sort of legislative monument which was commented on in the

(o) This point of view explains how it was that they deemed it useful, first, to indicate in the Code, after the original constitutions, the contents of the most recent Novels which had modified them: (these are the extracts known as the *Authentica*, from the name by which they themselves designated them, which long remained incorporated with the constitutions in the current editions of the *Corpus Juris Civilis*, but are rightly excluded from the scientific modern editions) ; and, secondly, to add to the *Corpus* a certain number of documents such as the *libri feudorum* which are not of Roman origin, and which are, as properly, excluded from the same editions.

schools, and cited before the tribunals, in the place of Justinian's compilations.

All direct study of the sources is conspicuously absent in the diffusive treatises, encumbered with subtleties and useless divisions, in which the later jurisconsults applied to the exposition of the law the processes of the scholastic dialectic. In point of fact, law did not on that account remain stationary any more than at any other period. The authors of this crude literature, which grew prolifically from the fourteenth century to the sixteenth,—the post-glossators, or the Bartolists, as they are called after the name of the most celebrated amongst them, the Italian Bartolus of Sasso Ferrato (1314-1357), and amongst whom the best known have been, besides Bartolus, his master Cino of Pistoia, then Baldus, Paul de Castro, Jason de Mayno, &c.,—did, under the pretext of Roman law, construct much new law; and this is the explanation of the influence acquired by them, not only in Italy, but in France and Germany(p), and throughout nearly the whole of learned Europe, where they exercised an almost exclusive domination, down to the sixteenth century(q). In this respect, they have played a considerable rôle in the general his-

(p) On the reception of Roman law in Germany, see amongst others, Dernburg, *Pandekten*, 1, p. 4 *et seq.*, and the authors cited.

(q) Savigny's volume six is dedicated to the Bartolists. See also Flach, *N. R. Hist.*, 1883, p. 218 *et seq.*; Esmein, p. 767 *et seq.*; Brissaud, p. 213 *et seq.*

tory of law. But they have played none in that of the science of Roman law properly so-called.

In the sixteenth century, on the other hand, a new period begins for Roman law, as a result of the revival of classical studies(r). The same movement, which had recalled to the attention of men the other monuments of antiquity, conduced to the study of the juridical monuments, which were no longer to be treated after the fashion of the glossators, as isolated documents, and in their latest form,—in their quality as positive law which must be taken in its most recent material expression,— but as a branch of ancient tradition which must be reconstituted in its purest form, by seeking to restore their original form and sense to the documents preserved in Justinian's compilations, and by employing side by side with them, as being instruments of equal value, the information derived from extra-juridical literature, and the texts of the ante-Justinian law recently rescued from oblivion.

This movement, the ultimate tendency of which was to restore the Roman law in its historical verity, instead of trying to interpret it in its legal definitive form, had

(r) See in general on this period, Esmein, p. 769 et seq.; Brissaud, p. 347 et seq.; Stintzing, *Geschichte des Rechtswissenschaft in Deutschland*, 1, 1880, pp. 307-385; A. Tardif, *Histoire des sources du droit français, origines romaines*, 1890, p. 464 et seq. Very complete lists of the jurisconsults of this period and of the following will also be found in Rivier, *Introduction historique*, p. 583 et seq.

for its precursor the Italian Andrea Alciati (1492-1540),
—professor successively at Avignon, Bourges, Pavia,
Bologna, and Ferrara,—along with whom is often mentioned with justice the Parisian Hellenist Budaeus (1467-
1540), and the German, Ulrich Zasius, professor at Frei-
burg in Brisgau (1461-1535) (s). Its most illustrious
representative was the great French Romanist, Jacques
Cujas(t), who was born at Toulouse in 1522, and died
in 1590; who lectured principally at Valence and Bourges, and had as pupils an immense number of celebrated
men of all countries; a jurisconsult of the old school,
who united in the highest degree the juridical sense,
properly so called, with the critical sagacity˙and the

(s) Of the three, Zasius alone has been the subject of a really
learned monograph (Stintzing, *Ulrich Zasius*, 1857. See also the
same writer's, *Gesch. d. Rechtswiss.*, 1, pp. 155-172); Bremer,
Z. S. St., 18, 1897; Germ. Abth., p. 170 *et seq.*

(t) The best work on Cujas still remains, in spite of its antiquated form, that of Berriat Saint-Prix, *Histoire du droit romain
suivie de l'histoire de Cujas*, 1812, which subsequent work
has done little more than appropriate. Spangenberg's German
translation, *J. Cujas und seine Zeitgenossen*, 1822, contains
moreover, besides some notes, a convenient bibliography of the
works of Cujas, pp. 231-307. Savigny's letter, *Themis*, 4, 1822,
pp. 194-207, also contains some important additions. *Opera
omnia*, edited by A. Fabrot in 10 vols., Paris, 1658. In greater
demand are the Naples reprints, 1722-1727, and those of Venice,
1758-1783, in 11 vols., not for the sake of a few mediocre additions, but because they are the most convenient for reference in
connection with a general index in two volumes, entitled *Promptu-
arium operum Jac. Cujacii auctore Dom. Albanensi*, 2 vols., 1763,
2nd ed., 1795.

philological and historical knowledge necessary to a perfectly intelligent interpretation of the Roman law. Among his numerous works, all of which are devoted to the exegetical study of the sources, the most import-ant are (besides some very good and learned editions of texts previously unpublished, or published in a defective manner), 28 books of *observationes* and *emendationes*, giv-ing, in a disorderly way, a mass of interpretations, cor-rections, restorations, or conjectures; also many works, in the main the outcome of his teaching, which aim at re-establishing in their original form, and expounding in their original sense, the fragmentary extracts from the writings of Roman jurisconsults, which form the compil-ations of Justinian (*tractatus ad Africanum,* commen-taries on Papinian, *recitationes sollemnes* on Paulus, Ul-pian, Marcellus, Julianus, Cervidius Scaevola, &c.).

In contrast to Cujas we must mention his adversary and only serious rival, Hugues Doneau (born in 1527, at Chalon-sur-Saône, professor at Bourges, and later, after being driven from France on account of his religious ideas, at Heidelberg, at Leyden, and at Altdorf, near Nuremberg, where he died in 1591), who is especially distinguished in that very domain of juridical science which Cujas abstained from entering upon (that of sys-tematic generalisations), and whose *Commentarii juris civilis* have remained for centuries very nearly the best methodical exposition of Roman law(*u*).

(*u*) Eyssal, *Doneau, sa vie et ses ouvrages*, 1860. Add Stint-zing, *Doneau in Altdorf*, 1869; H. Buhl, *Doneau in Heidelberg*,

I will mention, in addition:—Francois Le Douaren (Duarenus), born at Moncontour (Côtes-du-Nord) in 1509, died at Bourges in 1559, a pupil of Alciati, Doneau's master, and like him an opponent of Cujas, prior to whom he had delivered lectures at Bourges strongly marked by the new spirit; François Baudouin (Balduinus, 1520-1573), the author of good historical works, and much involved in the religious strifes of his period; the learned Barnabé Brisson (1531-1591); the two brothers Pithiou, Pierre (1539-1596), and François (1534-1621), pupils and very close friends of Cujas; the jurisconsult and philologist, Hubertus Giphanius (van Giffen, 1534-1616), who taught principally in Germany, but who belongs to the French school by his masters and his scientific affinities(v). Then other learned contemporaries, who on the contrary always remained strangers to this school, though following parallel lines:—at the very beginning of the movement, in Germany, Haloander (Gregorius Meltzer, 1501-1531) is still justly famous for the Noric editions of Justinian's collections published at Nuremberg in 1529-1531(w); in the Netherlands, Viglius Zuichemus, (so called from the town of Zwickem, near which he was

---

Neue Heidelberger Jahrbücher, 2, 1892, pp. 280-313; Opera omnia, Lucca, 1762-1770, for example.

(v) Stintzing, Gesch. d. Rechtswiss, 1, p. 405-414.

(w) Stintzing, pp. 180-203. See ibid., p. 209 et seq., on the Bâle editors.

born in 1507), who died in 1577, and was the first editor
of the Theophilus paraphrase(x); in Spain, the Bishop
of Tarragona, Antonius Augustinus (1516-1586), who
was, with Cujas, the principal restorer of the Greek constitutions of the Code(y); lastly, the Genevan professor,
born in Paris, Denis Godefroy (D. Gothofredus, 1549-
1622), whom I mention last because his edition of the
Corpus juris civilis has proved, in a measure, for the
work of the Romanists of the sixteenth century, what the
Great Gloss had been for the work of the glossators,—the
vehicle which has brought the results attained by it within
practical reach(z).

In the seventeenth and eighteenth centuries we
still meet remarkable interpreters of Roman law:
—in Savoy, President Favre (Antonius Faber, 1557-
1624), a great discoverer of Tribonianisms, whom the new
vogue for researches into interpolations has brought
again into note; at Geneva, Jacques Godefroy, son of
Denis (1587-1652), author of a masterly commentary on
the Theodosian code, who, by reason of his national and
scientific affiliations, may be reckoned among the great
French Romanists, and, in any case, is much more deserv-

(x) Stintzing, pp. 220-228.

(y) The most recent biography is in Maassen, *Geschichte der
Quellen und der Litteratur des canonischen Rechts*, 1, 1870, pp.
XIX-XXXIV. As to his value as a philologist, which is sometimes
a little overstated, cf. Ch. Graux, *Essai sur les origines du fonds
greo de l'Escurial*, 1880, pp. 13-17. *Opera omnia*, Lucca, 1765-
1774.

(z) Stintzing, pp. 386-388, and on his edition of the *Corpus,*
ibid., pp. 208-209.

ing of the name of Romanist, than the civilians Domat (1625-1696) and Pothier (1699-1772); in Germany, J. T. Heineccius (1681-1741), author of valuable works on the history of Roman law; lastly, in Holland, the members of the school which was the most worthy successor of the French school of the sixteenth century:—Ant. Vinnius (1558-1657), Jan Voet (1647-1713), Gérard Noodt (1647-1725), Ant. Schulting (1659-1734), Cornelius van Bynkershoek (1659-1743), &c. But we have there rather the last reflections of a vanished light, than the beginning of a new one.

The renaissance came in the nineteenth century in the country which had remained on the whole the greatest stranger to the grand awakening of the sixteenth century, —in Germany; and this time again it was the result of a general revival of the studies of philology and history. It is perhaps possible to find precursors of it:—for example, the old historian of Roman law, G. Hugo (1764-1844). But its direct promoter and most brilliant representative was the illustrious Frederick Charles von Savigny (who was born at Frankfort-on-the-Maine, in 1779, was professor at Berlin from 1810 to 1842, then minister of the Prussian Government up to 1848, and who died in 1861), author of the *System of Roman Law* (unfinished), (*System des heutigen römischen Rechts*), of the *Treatise on Possession* (*Das Recht des Besitzes*), and of the *History of Roman Law in the Middle Ages* (*Geschichte des römischen Rechts im Mittelalter*) (*a*), and founder of the historical school.

This school, which has given new life to the science of Roman law during our century, owed its strength to an axiom, the credit for formulating which, and acting upon it from the very first, must be conceded to Savigny:— the axiom, namely, that the law of a people is an historical product, and not something accidental and arbitrary; and that, consequently, an understanding of Roman law can only be attained by that combination of general views and erudite researches of a technical character which is the essential condition of all serious historical study. Thus Savigny's work forms the point of departure of all the marvellous development which has taken place since his time, down to the present, especially in Germany, and which is certainly not yet ended. No doubt, the researches of which he set the example with a rare mastery, with a singular understanding of the texts, and with an astonishing knowledge of the most diverse authorities in print and in manuscript, have been continued after him, and sometimes in opposition to him, to such a degree as to leave those who would still believe

(*a*) There are French translations of the first named works: (*Traité de droit romain,* tr. Guenoux, 8 vols., 1851-1855; *Traité de la possession,* translated from the 7th German eaition by H. Staedler, 1866) and of the first volumes of the third (translation by Guenoux, 3 vols., 1839). Another work of Savigny, *Le droit des obligations,* has been translated by Gerardin and Jozon, 2 vols., 2nd ed., 1873.

all knowledge included in his works as much strangers to the truth as were the post-glossators who concentrated themselves on the contemplation of the Gloss. No doubt also, the activity of Savigny and of his contemporaries was materially seconded by the discoveries of new texts, which form a fresh point of resemblance between the Renaissance of the sixteenth and that of the nineteenth centuries. But in this instance, as in the sixteenth century, it would be puerile to take the effect for the cause: documents till then unknown were discovered in the time of Savigny, as in that of Cujas, precisely because the revival of scientific curiosity stimulated the search for them. The discovery of the Verona manuscript of the Institutes of Gaius dates from 1816, and Savigny's method is already shewn, complete and perfect, in the first edition of his Treatise on Possession, published in 1803. If, on the other hand, Savigny has made some applications of his method which we look upon as mistaken; if he has sometimes allowed himself to be carried away by the seductions of a too rigorous dialectic; if, more often, as is the melancholy fate of works of learning, the very pursuit of the researches inaugurated by him has overturned the provisional explanatory theories which he deduced from his first discoveries—it is none the less true that all those who in our day have scientifically studied Roman law have been beneficially affected by his labours, and this is true even of those who have most vigorously opposed certain of his conceptions and methods; it is true even of him whose opposite qualities, whose robust sense of actual life and of juridical realities have rendered him most dangerous to the logical and cold deductions of Savigny,—the illustrious Ihering himself, who also enjoyed a long career, and exercised a powerful influence(b), and whom alone I advisedly mention here, side by side with the author of the System of Roman Law, among all the Romanists of the century(c).

(b) Besides *Der Geist des römischen Rechts*, which remains his principal work, a certain number of other works of Ihering which I cite in their place have been translated by Meulenaere.

(o) An extended enumeration of the Romanists of the century, dead before 1881, will be found in Rivier, *Introduction*, pp. 623-637. Salkowski's *Institutionen*, pp. 65-66, gives, in certain directions, some interesting characteristics of the German Romanists Haubold (1766-1824), Hasse (1779-1830), Puchta (1798-1846), Muehlenbruch (1785-1843), Dirksen (1790-1868), Keller (1799-1860), Vangerow (1808-1870), Boecking (1802-1870), Rudorff (1803-1873), Waechter (1797-1880), Bruns (1816-1880), Huschke (1801-1886), Brinz (1820-1887), Ihering (1818-1892), and Windschied (1817-1892), to whom were added a little later the names of Alfred Pernice (1841-1901), of Théodore Mommsen (1817-1903), and of Otto Karlowa (1836-1904).

APPENDIX.

GENERAL BIBLIOGRAPHY.*

I shall indicate in connection with each subject of discussion the works specially relating to it; and I call attention in my first book to the principal original sources of Roman law, which have come down to us. It will not, however, be out of place to give at once some general information about the collections and the works of a comprehensive character to which my principal references relate, indicating the abbreviations used in these references, and distinguishing in my enumeration the original sources, the commentaries, and the auxiliary works of reference relating either to other branches of Roman antiquities, or to the history of other systems of law, which may be profitably compared with Roman law.

I—Original Sources.

1. The fundamental documents are in every case the compilations made by order of the Emperor Justinian, and spoken of collectively as the *Corpus juris civilis* :—the

* The translators have deemed it more satisfactory to give the General Bibliography in its entirety, than to abbreviate or alter it in any way.

Digest, the Code, the Institutes, and the Novels. My references are to the excellent edition provided in portable shape by Mommsen, P. Krueger, Schoell and Kroll (*Corpus juris civilis, editio stereotypa: I. Institutiones, recognovit P. Krueger; Digesta, recognovit Th. Mommsen*, 1872. *II. Codex Justinianus, recognovit P. Krueger*, 1879. *III. Novellae, recognovit R. Schoell; absolvit G. Kroll*, 1880-1895).

As to the methods of citation, the references to the Novels are made by the number of the Novel, and, if necessary, the chapter: *Nov.* 17, *c.* 1=Novel 17, chapter 1: those to the Institutes are made by the numbers of the book, the title, and the paragraph, in addition to which I have also mentioned, for greater clearness, the abridged rubric of the title (*Inst.*, 3, 23, *De empt. vend.*, 3=Institutes, book 3, title 23, *De emptione venditione*, §3). As to the Digest, and the Code, one method, which is still the one most in vogue, indicates first the law, and if necessary, the paragraph, then the book and the title, to which is often added the rubric of the latter: (L. or Fr. 2, §32, *D.*, 1, 2, *De o.j.*=Law or fragment 2, §32, of title 2, of book 1 of the Digest, entitled *De origine juris; L.* or *C.* 3, *C.*, 5, 38, *De per. tut.*=Law or constitution 3 of title 38, of book 5 of the Code, entitled *De periculo tutorum.*) I have preferred, with some of the best modern authorities, a mode of citation which is simpler, more logical, and more in conformity with the methods followed in the case of literary texts, according to which the first number refers to the book, the second to the title, (of which here again I have indicated the rubric,) the third to the law, and the fourth, if necessary, to the paragraph: (*D.*, 1, 2, *De o.j.*, 1, 32; *C.* 5, 38, *De per. tut.*, 3.) In the case of several consecutive citations, the import of different figures may readily be understood by noticing that the abbreviated rubrics follow in every case, as a matter of course, the numbers of the titles, and that the references to the laws contained in one and the same title are separated by semicolons (*D.*, 1, 2, *De o.j.*, 1; 2), and those to the paragraphs of one and the same matter of law by full stops (*D.*, 1, 2, *De o.j.*, 2, 32. 33). Lastly, there will in like manner be no difficulty in understanding the more elliptical references made by the signs *D., h.t.; C., h.t.; Inst., h.t.;* to the titles of the Digest, Code, or Institutes indicated previously more at large, *i.e.*, as a rule, those referred to at the head of a section as constituting the principal sources. The numbers indicated in some places in parentheses relate to the different numbering of the older editions.

2. There exists, furthermore, a considerable number of fragments of Roman jurisconsults which have come down to us, but are not included in Justinian's compilations, of which collections have been made. The best is the *collectio* of Krueger, Mommsen and Studemund (*Collectio librorum juris antejustiniani, ediderunt P. Krueger, Th. Mommsen, G. Studemund: I. Gai. institutiones ediderunt P. Krueger and G. Studemund, ed. 4,*

1900. II. Ulpiani liber singularis regularum, Pauli libri quinque sententiarum, fragmenta minora saeculorum p. Chr. n. secundi et tertii recensuit Paulus Krueger, 1878. III. Fragmenta Vaticana, Mosaicarum et Romanarum legum collatio recognovit Theodorus Mommsen, Consultatio veteris cujusdam juris consulti, codices Gregorianus et Hermogenianus, alia minora edidit Paulus Krueger, 1890, 3 vols. 8vo), besides which it may sometimes be necessary to cite for the notes and discussions, the *Jurisprudentia* of Huschke (*Jurisprudentiae antejustinianae quae supersunt. Composuit Ph. Eduardus Huschke, ed. 5,* 18mo, 1886. Kübler et Seckel are preparing a sixth ˚ed., of which the Institutes of Gaius have already appeared in 1903); or, also especially for the discussions the collection of Bremer, *Jurisprudentia antehadriana,* 18mo, 1896-1901.

3. In connection with the collections coming under these two categories, reference must be made to: (*a*) the *Palingenesia juris civilis* of Lenel, 2 vols. 4to., 1889, (Lenel, *Pal.*), where the author, continuing the work begun in his restoration of the edict (Lenel, *Das Edictum perpetuum: ein Versuch zu dessen Wiederherstellung,* large 8vo, 1883=Lenel, *Ed.*), has rearranged in their natural order the texts of jurisconsults which have come down to us in fragmentary shape in the Digest, or elsewhere (exclusive of the Institutes of Gaius, the Sentences of Paulus, and the Rules of Ulpian). A few texts which may be profitably consulted in the *Palingenesia*

have been indicated between parentheses by the name of Lenel, and the number which they bear in his restoration of the work of their author. Thus the reference to Ulpian, *D.*, 6, 1, *De R.V.*, 68 (Lenel, 2987) signifies that the text is numbered 2987 in the restoration of the work of Ulpian given in the *Palingenesia.—(b)* The *Vocabularium jurisprudentiae Romanae editum jussu instituti Savigniani*, 4to, Vol. 1, A-C, 1894-1903.

4. One may have to consult, side by side with the constitutions contained in Justinian's Code, the Imperial Constitutions contained in the earlier Codes, (the Theodosian Code=*C. Th.*; the Gregorian Code=*C. Greg.*; the Hermogenian Code=*C. Herm.*,) for which the modern edition is that of Haenel, *Codices Theodosianus, Gregorianus, Hermogenianus*, ed. Haenel, 1842. *Appendix*, 1844, 4to. (See, nevertheless, as to the Gregorian and Hermogenian Codes, the observation on p. 155, note *m*). I refer to these Codes in the same way as to the Justinian Code: *C. Th.*, 1, 4, *De resp. prud.*, 3=Theodosian Code, book 1, title 4, *De responsis prudentium*, constitution or law 3.

5. Inscriptions have preserved for us a large quantity of juridical documents. The general collection of Latin inscriptions is the *Corpus inscriptionum Latinarum*, published since the year 1863, in folio volumes by the Berlin Academy (*C.I.L.*), along with which I have sometimes had occasion to cite the *Ephemeris epigraphica* (large 8vo, 1873 et seq.=*Eph. ep.*), which is the periodical supplement of it; and the selections of Orelli-Hen-

zen (*Inscriptionum Latinarum amplissima collectio, ed. J. C. Orellius*, 1828; *vol. tertium, ed. Henzen*, 1856, 3 vols. 8vo), and of Dessau (*Inscriptiones Latinae selectae*, 2 vols. 8vo, 1892-1901).

There are also many documents relating to Roman law, not only among the Greek inscriptions (*Corpus inscriptionum Graecarum*, 4 vols., folio, Berlin, 1828-1877 =*C.I. Gr.*), but also in the Greek papyri of Egypt, the study of which has become quite a distinct branch of learning, having its special organ since 1900 in the *Archiv für Papyrusforschung*, and for which I have cited especially the recent collections of the Berlin Museum (*Aegyptische Urkunde aus den königlichen Museen zu Berlin, Griechische Urkunden*, I, 1895; II, 1898; III. 1903; IV, 1, 1904, folio=*G.B.U.*), the collection of the Archduke Renier at Vienna (*Corpus papyrorum Raineri, vol. I. Griechische Texte herausgegeben von C. Wessely, 1 Band, Rechtsurkunden, unter Mitwirkung von L. Mitteis*, 1895, folio=*C.P.R.*), of the British Museum (*Greek Papyri in the British Museum. Catalogue with texts, edited by F. G. Kenyon*, I, 1893. II, 1898, folio= *P. Lond.*), and that of the Oxyrhynchus papyrus published by Messrs. Grenfell and Hunt (*The Oxyrhynchus Papyri, edited with translations and notes by Bernard P. Grenfell and Arthur S. Hunt*, I, 1898; II, 1899; III, 1903; IV, 1904, 4to=*P. Oxy.*).

Lastly, there is a special collection of inscriptions relating to Roman law, namely, that of Bruns, brought down to date by Mommsen and Gradenwitz (Bruns, *Fontes=Fontes juris Romani antiqui ed. C. G. Bruns, ed. 6, cura Th. Mommseni et O. Gradenwitz, I, Leges et negotia,* 1893. The 2nd part, *II, Scriptores,* 1893, gives a certain number of literary texts interesting from their bearing upon the law) :

6. The text of the Institutes of Justinian, the extant fragments of jurisconsults not included in the compilations of Justinian, and the principal juridical inscriptions will be found collected with discussions and explanatory notes, in my *Textes de droit romain,* 3rd ed., 1903, 18mo. (=*Textes*).

II.—Commentaries.

The literature directly relating to Roman law includes, besides certain periodical reviews, histories of the sources, general histories of Roman law, and treatises on private law, which are, in some countries, themselves subdivided into Pandect treatises and Institute treatises.

1. As to the treatises on private law (which it is all the more essential to make special mention of here, because, except for certain special points, I have refrained from making constant references to them in connection with different matters which we treat of in common), I shall cite, in the case of France, besides Ortolan's work which is already old, but still remarkable for its lively

style of exposition, and made complete by some appendices due to Labbé (Ortolan, *Législation romaine, I, Histoire et généralisation*, 12th ed., 1884; *II, III, Explication historique des Instituts*, 12th ed., 1883, 3 vols., 1883-1884), the finished treatise of Accarias (Accarias, *Précis de droit romain*, 4th ed., 2 vols., 8 vo., Paris, 1886-1891), and two recent manuals of Gaston May (*Eléments de droit romain*, 7th ed., 1901) and of Petit (*Traité éléméntaire de droit romain*, 4th ed., 1903).

In the case of Germany especially, though not exclusively, one must distinguish between the Institute treatises, where Roman law is expounded in a summary and especially historical way, and the Pandect treatises in which it is studied in a more dogmatic and detailed manner.

(*a*) Among the Institute manuals, I would particularly commend the now old work of Puchta, supplemented by the abundant notes of Rudorff, and since brought down to date by Paul Krueger (Puchta, *Kursus der Institutionen, 10 Auflage besorgt von P. Krueger*, 2 vols. 8vo., 1893); Salkowski's book, which is very remarkable for the happy selection of texts cited as authorities (Salkowski, *Lehrbuch der Institutionen, 7th Aufl.* 1898); the very clear and very precise book of Baron (Baron, *Geschichte des römischen Rechts, I, Institutionen und Civilprozess*, 1884); and the work, which has speedily become popular on account of its fervour and its attractive style, of Sohm (R. Sohm, *Institutionen des*

römischen Rechts, 8-9 Aufl. 1899) ; and, lastly, that of
Leonhard (*Institutionen des römischen Rechts*, 1894),
which is, so far as I know, the latest which has appeared.
In spite of its restriction to a determinate period, which
is expressed in its title, we may compare with the most
extended of these manuals of Institutes, the English
work of Roby, *Roman Private Law in the times of Cicero
and of the Antonines*, 2 vols., 1902.

(*b*) The most complete Pandect treatise, that in
which one will be most certain to find any question discussed and the bibliography of it, is, in my opinion, that
of B. Windscheid, *Lehrbuch des Pandektenrechts* (3
vols., 1891; Italian translation by Bensa and Fadda),
which has been brought down to date and into correla-
tion with the articles of the new German Code, in an
8th edition, published by Th. Kipp, 3 vols., 1900-1901. The
justly popular work of Dernburg (*Pandekten*, I, 6th
ed., 1900; II, 6th ed., 1903; III, 5th ed., 1894), gives
a vivacious exposition of the principal points, accompanied
by a large amount of historical information. That of
Brinz (*Lehrbuch der Pandekten, 2 Aufl.*, 1873-1892,
revised in its latter portions by Lotmar), is distinguished by great originality and rare acuteness. The
Pandects of Baron (*Pandekten, 9 Aufl.*, 1896), shew
in their concise form the same precision and the same
clearness as do his Institutes. The Pandects of Vangerow (*Lehrbuch der Pandekten*, 7th ed. unaltered, 3 vols.,
1867), which are not an exact treatise, but a skeleton out-

line accompanied by dissertations upon questions arbitrarily selected, nevertheless furnish models of juridical discussion upon those questions. I shall mention, in addition, the two volumes already published of the *System des heutigen Pandektenrechts,* of Bekker, 1886, 1889; next, especially for the sake of the Italian translation with notes which has been made of it by Serafini, the Pandects of Arndts (*Pandekten, 13 Aufl., besorgt von Pfaff and Hofmann,* 1886; *Trattato di Pandette di Arndts, ed. 4,* 1882); and as one of the latest and most complete, that of Regelsberger, of which only Division 1 has appeared (*Pandekten, 1,* 1893, in Binding, *Handbuch der deutschen Rechtswissenschaft*). I will end with the *Manuale di Pandette,* a very learned work, and full of matter despite its small size, of C. Ferrini, of which a second edition has just been published by Baviera (1 vol., 1904).

In this list of Pandect treatises, I must also make special mention of the colossal work of Glück, *Ausführliche Erläuterung der Pandekten,* 1797 *et seq.* (Italian translation in course of preparation) commenced at the end of the last century and still unfinished, and yet even now constituting a library of which the oldest parts are a little antiquated, but of which, on the other hand, the recent parts are sometimes exceedingly important. To it I will add, notwithstanding their slightly different character, the works treating of our subject in a general way, of Savigny (*System des heutigen römischen Rechts,* incomplete, French translation by Guenoux, 7 vols., 1851-1855), of Ihering *Geist des römischen Rechts* (*Esprit du droit romain*=*Esp. du Dr. r.*, translated by Meulenaere, 3rd ed., 4 vols., 1886, 1887, 1888; my references are to the first edition, 1880), and of Pernice (*Marcus Antistius Labeo, Römisches Privatrecht im 2 Jahrhunderte der Kaiserzeit*, I, 1873; II, 1878; II, 1, 2nd ed. 1895; II, 2, 2nd ed., 1900; III,.1, 1892=Pernice, *Labeo*, 1; 2; 2,1; 2, 2; 3, 1).

(2) As to the books devoted either to the history of the law or solely to the history of the sources, there exists for the history of the sources an excellent work: it is *Geschichte der Quellen und Litteratur des römischen Rechts* (*Histoire des sources du droit romain*), published by Paul Krueger in Binding's Manual, and of which a French translation has been added by Brissaud to the translation of Mommsen and Marquardt's *Manuel d'antiquités romaines* (=Krueger, *Sources*). There should now be added to these the more concise and more recent work of Kipp, *Geschichte der Quellen des römischen Rechts*, 2nd ed., 1903. Two of the latest general histories of Roman law, but very different from each other in point of magnitude and character, are the unfinished work of Otto Karlowa (*Römische Rechtsgeschichte von Otto Karlowa*, I: *Staatsrecht und Rechtsquellen*: II: *Privatrecht*, &c., 1885-1902=Karlowa, *R.R.G.*); and that of Schulin (*Lehrbuch der Geschichte des römischen Rechts*, small 8vo, 1889=Schulin, *Lehrbuch*) especially remarkable for its numerous comparisons with Greek and

Oriental law. *Römische Rechtsgeschichte* by Moritz Voigt, (I, 1892; II, 1899; III, 1902; 8vo), affords, with numerous references to the former works of the author, a good specimen of his sometimes rather surprising theories and method. The ideas upon the history of the sources and of Roman law, advanced by Bruns and afterwards reviewed and largely rearranged by Pernice, and afterwards by Lenel, in Holtzendorff's Encyclopædia (Holtzendorff, *Encyclopädie der Rechtswissenschaft, I, 6 Aufl.*, 1904, pp. 77—170A=Bruns-Lenel, *Gesch. und Quell.*) form, in my opinion, a work of prime importance. *L'Introduction historique au droit romain* of Rivier, 2nd ed. 1889 (= Rivier, *Introduction*) gives much information in the form of a skeleton outline with references. I also cite, especially on account of the information given about certain foreign works by the translator's appendices, Muirhead's book, *Historical Introduction to the Private Law of Rome*, translated by Bourcart, 1889. Lastly, I think I ought to class among treatises on the history of the private law, because of its chronological arrangement, the work of Cuq, *Les institutions juridiques des Romains*, 2 vols., 1891-1902.

(3) The legal periodicals to which I have oftenest had occasion to refer are: in France, the *Nouvelle Revue historique de droit français et étranger* (=*N.R. hist.*), 8vo, 1877 *et seq.*, and the *Revue générale du droit* (=*R. gén.*), 8vo. 1877 *et seq.*; in Italy, the *Archivio giuridico*, 8vo, 1867 *et seq.* (=*Archivio*), the *Bul-*

lettino dell'istituto di diritto Romano (=*Bull. dell'ist di D.R.*), 1888 *et seq.;* in Germany, the *Zeitschrift für geschichtliche Rechtswissenschaft* (=*Z.G.R.*), 15 vols. 8vo, 1815-1850, the *Zeitschrift für Rechtsgeschichte* (= *Z.R.G.*), 13 vols. 8vo, 1862-1878, a continuation of the preceding, and the *Zeitschrift der Savigny-Stiftung für Rechtsgeschichte, Romanistische Abtheilung* (=*Z.S.St.*), 8vo, 1880 *et seq.,* which is a continuation of the other two; the *Zeitschrift für privat-und öffentliches Recht,* published in Vienna by Professor Grünhut since 1878 (Grünhut's *Zeitschrift*); the *Jahrbücher für Dogmatik des heutigen römischen und deutschen Privat-rechts,* founded in 1857 by Gerber and von Ihering (Ihering's *Jahrbücher*); the *Archiv für civilistische Praxis,* 1818 *et seq.* (=*Archiv*); and the *Kritische Vierteljahresschrift für Gesetzgebung und Rechtswissenschaft* of Munich (=*K.V.I.*), 1856 *et seq.*

III.—AUXILIARY WORKS OF REFERENCE.

As for other auxiliary works of reference, relating either to other branches of Roman antiquities, or to other systems of law, it would be as easy as it would be of little profit, to set forth here extended inventories of them. I shall confine myself to indicating in a purely practical way the works to which I have oftenest referred, or which seem to me likely to prove the most worth consulting in the matter, on the one hand, of public law, Roman history, Roman chronology, and the history of Latin literature, &c., and on the other hand, of the history of comparative law.

(1) For public law I have especially referred to the French translation of Mommsen's standard work *Römisches Staatsrecht* (*Le droit public romain*, 7 parts in 8 vols, 8vo, 1889-1895=Mommsen *Dr. publ.*). I have also sometimes cited the shorter work by the same author, since published in Binding's Manual (*Abriss des römischen Staatsrecht*, 1893=Mommsen, *Abriss*), where some new points are touched upon, notably for the Byzantine period, which is not included in the large work. Willem's *Le droit public romain*, 5th ed., 1888, may be also mentioned for the sake of the bibliography.

Most of my references for Roman history are again to the French translation of Mommsen's *Roman History* (*Hist. Rom.*), made for the first three volumes of the German work by Alexandre (8 vols., 8vo, 1863-1873), and for the fifth, by Cagnat and Toutain (3 vols., 8vo, 1887-1889). Beyond that, I have generally dispensed with further bibliography, by referring to the résumé, very short, but full of individuality and of information, given by Niese, *Abriss der römischen Geschichte von B. Niese* (2nd ed., 1897=Niese, *Abriss*).

For the Roman .chronology,—on the theoretical difficulties of which the most up-to-date French work is an article of Bouché-Leclerq, published in the *Revue historique*, vol. 42, 1890, pp. 398-415 (see the same also in Daremberg and Saglio, v. *Fasti*),—the two books of practical reference which I have especially used are, for the period of the Republic, that, now old but not replaced, of J. C. Fischer, *Römische Zeittafeln*, 4to, 1844, and for the Empire, that of Georges Goyau, *Chronologie de l'Empire romain*, 18mo., 1891.

For the history of Latin literature, I have been especially assisted by the works of Teuffel, *Geschichte der römischen Litteratur, 5 Aufl. bearbeitet von L. Schwabbe*, 2 vols. 8vo, 1890 (there exists a French translation from a previous edition), and of Schanz, *Geschichte der römischen Litteratur*, I, 2nd ed., 1898; II, 2nd ed., 1899-1901; IV, 1, 1904.

Lastly, it will suffice to say that the citations made, particularly for the system of names, from Cagnat, *Cours d'épigraphie*, refer to the work of René Cagnat, *Cours d'épigraphie latine*, 3rd ed., large 8vo, 1898; and that my references to Marquardt, *Culte, Vie privée*, etc., refer to the volumes of the French translation of Mommsen and Marquardt's, *Handbuch d. röm. Alterthümer* (*Manuel des antiquités romaines*), published in 1888 *et seq.*, to which also belong the translation of the *Droit public* of Mommsen and that of the *Histoire des sources* of Krueger. The reader will recognise with equal ease the citations from special reviews such as the *Hermes, Zeitschrift für klassische Philologie*, 8vo, 1866 *et seq.* (=*Hermes*), or from accumulations of learning such as the *Dictionnaire d'Antiquités grecques et romaines* of Daremburg and Saglio, 4to, Paris, 1872 *et seq.*, and the *Realencyclopädie der classischen Alter-thumswissenschaft,* of Pauly, Part I., 2nd ed., 1866, Parts 2-6, 1844, 6 vols., 8vo, of which a new edition edited by Wissowa (Pauly-Wissowa, *Realencyclopädie*) begun to appear in 1892.

(2) Roman law, viewed in its historical development, cannot be separated from the law of other people of like origin, nor even, if one regards juridical institutions as more than a mere accidental phenomenon, from that universal law the history of which constitutes what is called the history of comparative law. Possibly the comparative science of law is as yet incomplete. But it would be as unscientific systematically to neglect, on this pretext, the results already achieved, as it would be to accept without criticism all the hasty suggestions of generalisation. I believe that I have kept within the bounds of truth by bringing to bear on the main points the comparisons furnished by the institutions not only of the Indo-Europeans, (often restricted, indeed, to some Indo-Europeans), but of all races.

I have for the general history of the law, as well as for the special history of Indo-European races, principally cited the researches of Dareste, partly collected in his *Études d'histoire du droit,* 1889, and his *Nouvelles Études d'histoire du droit,* 1902, and those of Albert Hermann Post, of which a recent publication in convenient form is furnished by his *Grundriss der ethnologischen Jurisprudenz,* 2 vols. 18mo, 1894-1895, and the numerous articles contributed especially by Kohler, Bernhoeft and Dargun, to the excellent *Zeitschrift für vergleichende Rechtswissenschaft* (*Zeitschr. für vergl. R.W.*) founded in 1878 by Bernhoeft and Cohn, and carried on since Part 3 by Bernhoeft, Cohn and Kohler. I have also more than once referred to the works of Sumner Maine (*Ancient Law*, 1861; *Early Institutions*, 1875; *Early Law and Custom*, 1883), which, notwithstanding their rather wavering (*flottant*) and superficial character, have helped much to attract attention in France to the new science. Lastly, it would have been affectation on my part not to cite in appropriate places Fustel de Coulange's book on the *Cité antique*, 18mo, 14th., ed., 1895, and those of Leist on Aryan law (*Graeco-Italische Rechtsgeschichte*, 1884; *Altarisches jus gentium*, 1889; *Altarisches jus civile*, 1892). But I must add that they both ground themselves upon two master ideas against which the progress of knowledge is in my opinion constantly accumulating stronger and stronger objections:—on the one hand, the idea that one can reproduce the original institutions of the Indo-Europeans by taking certain arbitrarily selected groups, and by neglecting more or less frankly certain others, such as the Germans and the Slavs; and on the other hand, the idea that the religious books of India, and especially the Rig-Veda, represent the primitive condition of Hindoo civilisation. As against the first idea, Schrader, *Sprachvergleichung und Urgeschichte*, 2nd ed., 1890, and the post-

humous, recently translated work of Ihering, *Les Indo-*
Européens avant l'histoire, 1895, (*Vorgeschichte der*
Indoeuropäer) may be profitably consulted; as against
the second, the remarks of the German editor of Ihering's
work, p. VII *et seq.*

As to the different concrete systems of law, I have
especially referred, for the history of Greek law, to
Dareste, Haussoullier, and Reinach, *Recueil des inscrip-*
tions juridiques grecques), I, 1891-1894, II, fasc., *1*
1898 (=Dareste, Haussoullier, Reinach, *Inscr. juridiques*
grecques), and to Beauchet, *Histoire du droit privé de*
la République athénienne, 4 vols., 1897; for the history
of Egyptian law to the researches of Revillout, (*Les*
obligations en droit égyptien, 1886; *La propriété, ses*
démembrements, et la possession en droit égyptien, 1897,
&c.); for the history of Celtic law, to those of d'Arbois de
Jubainville, and in particular to his *Cours de droit celti-*
que, 2 vols. 8vo, Paris, 1875; for the history of Germanic
law, to H. Brunner, *Deutsche Rechtsgeschichte*, 2 vols.
8vo, 1887-1892 (=Brunner, *Deutsche Rechtsgesch.*) and
for the history of French law, to the works of Esmein
(*Cours élémentaire d'histoire du droit français*, 8vo, 4th
ed., 1901,=Esmein *Cours élémentaire*), Viollet (*Histoire*
du droit civil français, 2nd ed., 1893=Viollet, *Hist. du*
droit français), and Brissaud (*Manuel d'histoire du*
droit français, 2 vols., 1898-1904=Brissaud, *Manuel*).

INDEX.

Absolutio, 79,(*i*).
Accensi velati, 36.
Acknowledgments, 143, note.
Actio furti, 85 ;—*Pauliana,* 86,(*q*) ;—*Publiciana,* 86,(*q*) ;
. —*Rutiliana,* 86,(*q*).
Actiones fictitiae, 85 ;—*in factum,* 85-6;—*praetoriae,*
85-6.
Actions of the law, 28, 55-9.—See *Manus injectio;—*
Sacramentum;—Praetorian action.
Adgnati.—See Agnates.
Adjudicatio;—Part of *formula,* 79,(*i*).
Adoptio, 94.
Adpromissor, adpromissio. See *Sponsio.*
Adrogation, 31. 65.—See Adoption.
Aediles curules, 63. 83. 104. 111;—*plebis,* 45.
Aelianum, Jus, 96.
Aelius (Q.) Tubero, 98.
Aerarium, 63. 102. 104.
Aes et libra;—see *Nexum;*—Testament.
Africanus (Sex. Caecilius), 134.
Agere (of the Jurisconsults), 95.
Agnates, Agnation, 25-6.
Agrimensores, 142, note.
Album praetoris, 84.
Alciati, 178.
Alfenus Varus, 97.

Reprints of the Legal Classics Published by
The Lawbook Exchange, Ltd.

∞Admiralty & Maritime Law ∞

Flanders, Henry. [1824-1911]. *A Treatise on Maritime Law.* Boston: Little, Brown and Company, 1852. xvi, 444 pp. Reprinted 1999 by The Lawbook Exchange, Ltd. ISBN 1-886363-72-2. Cloth. $75.

Kulsrud, Carl J. *Maritime Neutrality to 1780. A History of the Main Principles Governing Neutrality and Belligerency to 1780.* Boston: Little, Brown, and Company, 1936. x, 351 pp. LC 99-38825. ISBN 1-58477-027-9. Reprint available March 2000 by The Lawbook Exchange, Ltd. Cloth. New. $65.

Marsden. R.[eginald]. G.[odfrey], ed. *Documents Relating to Law and Custom of the Sea.* [n.p.]: The Navy Record Society, 1915-6. Two volumes. xxxiii, 561; xl, 457, [5] pp. Reprinted 1999 by The Lawbook Exchange, Ltd. LCCN 99-24138. ISBN 1-886363-96-X. Cloth. $175.

[Twiss, Sir Travers]. *The Black Book of the Admiralty, with an Appendix.* Monumenta Juridica. Edited by Sir Travers Twiss. Four volumes. 4, xciii, 491, [2]; 4, lxxxvii, 500, 31; 4, lxxxvi, 673, [1], 31; 4, clii, 559, 32 pp. LCCN 97-38809 ISBN 1-886363-39-0. 1871. Reprinted 1998 by The Lawbook Exchange, Ltd. Cloth. $495.

∞ Law & Literature ∞

Barton, Dunbar Plunket. *Shakespeare and the Law.* With a foreword by James M. Beck. Boston: Houghton Mifflin Company, 1929. xl, 167 pp. Reprint available October 1999 by The Lawbook Exchange, Ltd. LCCN 99-26602. ISBN 1-58477-000-7. Cloth. $60.

Darrow, Clarence. *A Persian Pearl. And Other Essays.* East Aurora, NY: The Roycroft Shop, 1899. 175 pp. Reprinted 1997 by The Lawbook Exchange, Ltd. ISBN 1-886363-27-7. Cloth. $50.

Darrow, Clarence S. *An Eye for an Eye.* New York: Fox Duffield & Company, 1905. 213 pp. Reprinted 1996 by The Lawbook Exchange, Ltd. ISBN 1-886363-07-2. Cloth. $40.

Davis, C.K. *The Law in Shakespeare.* Washington, D.C.: Washington Law Book Co., [1883]. 303 pp. Reprinted 1999 by The Lawbook Exchange, Ltd. ISBN 1-886363-75-7. Cloth. $60.

Gest, John Marshall. *The Lawyer in Literature*. London: Sweet & Maxwell, Limited, 1913. xii, 249 pp. Reprint available November 1999 by The Lawbook Exchange, Ltd. LCCN99-18365. ISBN 1-886363-90-0. Cloth. $60.

Holdsworth, William S. *Charles Dickens as a Legal Historian*. New Haven: Yale University Press, 1929. 157 pp. Reprinted 1995 by The Lawbook Exchange, Ltd. ISBN 1-886363-06-4. Cloth. $40.

ℭ Legal Biography ℭ

Foss, Edward. *A Biographical Dictionary of the Judges of England From the Conquest to the Present Time 1066-1870*. London: John Murray, 1870. xv, 792 pp. Reprint available February 2000 by The Lawbook Exchange, Ltd. LCCN 99-12577. ISBN 10886363-86-2. Cloth. $100.

Richards, John T. *Abraham Lincoln The Lawyer-Statesman*. Boston: Houghton Mifflin, 1916. Frontis. Illustrated. xii, 260 pp. Reprint available November 1999 by The Lawbook Exchange, Ltd. LCCN 99-20587. ISBN 1-886363-94-3. Cloth. $60.

Townsend, William H. *Lincoln the Litigant*. Boston: Houghton Mifflin Company, 1925. [ix], [117] pp. Frontis. Illus. Reprint available February 2000 by The Lawbook Exchange, Ltd. LCCN 99-16499. ISBN 1-58477-021-X. Cloth. $60.

ℭ Legal Codes ℭ

[Field Codes]. [New York 1850-1865]. New York Field Codes. 1850-1865.
Vol. I. *The Code of Civil Procedure of the State of New-York, Reported Complete by the Commissioners on Practice and Pleadings. 1850.*
Vol. II. *The Code of Criminal Procedure of the State of New York, Reported Complete by the Commissioners on Practice and Pleadings. 1850.*
Vol. III. *The Civil Code of the State of New York, Reported Complete by the Commissioners of the Code. 1865.*
Vol. IV. *The Penal Code of the State of New York, Reported Complete by the Commissioners of the Code. 1865.*
Vol. V. *The Political Code of the State of New York. 1860.*
With a new introduction by Michael Weber. Reprinted 1998 by The Lawbook Exchange, Ltd. Five volume series. [8], xcvi, 791; liii, [1], 486; cxii, 776; lxiv, 406, clxvii; xlvii, 607 pp. ISBN 1-886363-40-4 (set). Cloth. $495.

Livingston, Edward. *A System of Penal Law, for the State of Louisiana: Consisting of A Code of Crimes and Punishments, A Code of Procedure, A Code of Evidence, A Code of Reform and Prison Discipline, A Book of Definitions. Prepared Under the Authority of a Law of the Said State. To Which are Prefixed a Preliminary Report on the Plan of a Penal Code, and Introductory Reports to the Several Codes Embraced in the System of Penal Law.* Philadelphia: James Kay, Jun. & Brother, 1833.v, 745 pp. Reprint available November 1999 by The Lawbook Exchange, Ltd. LCCN 99-11403. ISBN 1-886363-83-8. Cloth. $95.

ଔ Legal Dictionaries ଔ

Anderson, William C. *A Dictionary of Law, Consisting of Judicial Definitions and Explanations of Words, Phrases, and Maxims, and an Exposition of the Principles of Law: Comprising a Dictionary and Compendium of American and English Jurisprudence.* Chicago: T.H. Flood and Company, 1889. viii, 1140pp. Reprinted 1996 by The Lawbook Exchange, Ltd. ISBN 1-886363-23-4. Cloth. $125.

Black, Henry Campbell. *A Law Dictionary. Containing Definitions of the Terms and Phrases of American and English Jurisprudence, Ancient and Modern. And Including the Principal Terms of International, Constitutional, Ecclesiastical and Commercial Law, and Medical Jurisprudence, with a Collection of Legal Maxims, Numerous Select Titles from the Roman, Modern Civil, Scotch, French, Spanish, and Mexican Law, and Other Foreign Systems, and a Table of Abbreviations.* St. Paul, Minn.: West Publishing, 1910. 1314 pp. Reprinted 1995 by The Lawbook Exchange, Ltd. ISBN 1-886363-10-2. Cloth. $125.

Black, Henry Campbell. *A Dictionary of Law. Containing Definitions of the Terms and Phrases of American and English Jurisprudence, Ancient and Modern. Including the Principal Terms of International, Constitutional, and Commercial Law; with a Collection of Legal Maxims and Numerous Select Titles from the Civil Law and Other Foreign Systems.* St. Paul, Minn.: West Publishing, 1891. x, 1253 pp. Reprinted 1991 by The Lawbook Exchange, Ltd. ISBN 0-9630106-0-3. $125.

Bouvier, John. *A Law Dictionary Adapted to the Constitution and Laws of the United States of America, and of the Several States of the American Union; with References to the Civil and Other Systems of Foreign Law.* Philadelphia: T. & J.W. Johnson, 1839. Two volumes. 559; 28 pp. Reprinted 1993 by The Lawbook Exchange, Ltd. ISBN 0-9630106-7-0. Cloth. $130.

Burrill, Alexander M. *A New Law Dictionary and Glossary: Containing Full Definitions of the Principal Terms of the Common and Civil Law, Together with*

Translations and Explanations of the Various Technical Phrases in Different Languages, Occurring in the Ancient and Modern Reports, and Standard Treatises; Embracing Also All the Principal Common and Civil Law Maxims. Compiled on the Basis of Spelman's Glossary, and Adapted to the Jurisprudence of the United States; with Copious Illustrations, Critical and Historical. New York: John S. Voorhies, 1850. Two volumes. xviii, 1099 pp. Reprinted 1998 by The Lawbook Exchange, Ltd. LC 97-38481. ISBN 1-886363-32-3. Cloth. $175.

Holthouse, Henry James. *A New Law Dictionary, Containing Explanations of Such Technical Terms and Phrases As Defined in the Works of Legal Authors, in the Practice of the Courts, and in the Parliamentary Proceedings of the Houses of Lords and Commons, To Which Is Added An Outline of An Action at Law and of A Suit in Equity. Edited, from the Second and Enlarged London Edition, With Numerous Additions, by Henry Penington.* Philadelphia: Lea and Blanchard, 1847. viii, [17]-495 pp. Reprinted 1999 by The Lawbook Exchange, Ltd. ISBN 1-886363-67-6. Cloth. $75.

Jacob, Giles. [1686-1744]. *The Law-Dictionary: Explaining the Rise, Progress, and Present State of the English Law; Defining and Interpreting the Terms or Words of Art; and Comprising Copious Information on the Subjects of Law, Trade, and Government. Corrected and Greatly Enlarged by T[homas] E[dlyne] Tomlins.* New York: Printed for, and Published by I. Riley, 1811. Originally six volumes, viii, 531; [2], 543; [2],618; [2], 472; [2], 553; [2], 471pp. Reprint available January 2000 by The Lawbook Exchange, Ltd. ISBN 1-886363-68-4. Cloth. $495.

Rapalje, Stewart and Lawrence, Robert L. *A Dictionary of American and English Law with Definitions of the Technical terms of the Canon and Civil Laws. Also, Containing a Full Collection of Latin Maxims, and Citations of Upwards of Forty Thousand Reported Cases, in which Words and Phrases Have Been Judicially Defined or Construed.* Jersey City: Frederick C. Linn & Co., 1888. Two volumes. xxxviii, 1380 pp. Reprinted 1997 by The Lawbook Exchange, Ltd. LC 97-38484. ISBN 1-886363-33-1. Cloth. $195.

Stimson, Frederic Jesup. *Glossary of Technical Terms, Phrases, and Maxims of the Common Law.* Boston: Little, Brown, and Company, 1881. iv, 305pp. Reprinted 1999 by The Lawbook Exchange, Ltd. ISBN 1-886363-70-6. Cloth. $60.

Tayler, Thomas. *The Law Glossary: Being a Selection of the Greek, Latin, Saxon, French, Norman and Italian Sentences, Phrases, and Maxims, Found in the Leading English and American reports, and Elementary Works.* New York: Lewis & Blood, 1856. 580 pp. Reprinted 1995 by The Lawbook Exchange, Ltd. ISBN 1-886363-12-9. Cloth. $65.

೧ Legal History ೧

Bar, Carl Ludwig von. *A History of Continental Criminal Law.* Boston: Little, Brown, and Company, 1916. lvi, 561 pp. Reprint available October 1999 by The Lawbook Exchange, Ltd. LCCN 99-32341. ISBN 1-58477-013-9. Cloth. $90.

[Brandeis, Louis D.]. *Brandeis on Zionism. A Collection of Addresses and Statements by Louis D. Brandeis with a Foreword by Mr. Justice Felix Frankfurter.* Washington, D.C.: Zionist Organization of America, [1942]. viii, 156 pp. Reprinted 1999 by The Lawbook Exchange, Ltd. ISBN 1-886363-60-9. Cloth. $65.

Calhoun, George M. *The Growth of Criminal Law in Ancient Greece.* Berkeley: University of California Press, 1927. x, 149 pp. LC 99-43192. ISBN 1-58477-037-6. Reprint available December 1999 by The Lawbook Exchange, Ltd. Cloth. New. $50.

Corwin, Edward. *The Doctrine of Judicial Review: Its Legal and Historical Basis and Other Essays.* Princeton: Princeton University Press, 1914. ix, 178 pp. Reprint available December 1999 by The Lawbook Exchange, Ltd. LCCN 99-32362. ISBN 1-58477-011-2. Cloth. $60.

Darrow, Clarence and William J. Bryan. *The World's Most Famous Court Trial. Tennessee Evolution Case. A Complete Stenographic Report of the Famous Court Test of the Anti-Evolution Act, at Dayton July 10 to 21, 1925, Including Speeches and Arguments of Attorneys.* Cincinnati: National Book Company, [1925]. [4], 339 pp. Reprinted 1997 by The Lawbook Exchange, Ltd. LC 97-38485. ISBN 1-886363-31-5. Cloth. $65.

Dawson, John P. *A History of Lay Judges.* Cambridge, Mass.: Harvard University Press, 1960. viii, [2], 310 pp. Reprinted 1999 by The Lawbook Exchange, Ltd. ISBN 1-886363-69-2. Cloth. $75.

Evans, E.P. *The Criminal Prosecution and Capital Punishment of Animals.* New York: E.P. Dutton, 1906. x, 384pp. Reprinted 1998 by The Lawbook Exchange, Ltd. LC 98-12801. ISBN 1-886363-52-8. Cloth. $65.

Forsyth, William. *History of Trial by Jury [Second edition].* Jersey City: Frederick D. Linn, [1875]. x, 388 pp. Reprinted 1994 by The Lawbook Exchange, Ltd. ISBN 0-9630106-8-9. Cloth. $65.

Forsyth, William. *The History of Lawyers. Ancient and Modern.* Boston: Estes & Lauriat, 1875. Illustrated. xvii, 404 pp. Reprinted 1996 by the Lawbook Exchange, Ltd. ISBN 1-886363-14-5. Cloth. $60.

Fortescue, Sir John. [?1394-1476?]. *The Governance of England: Otherwise Called The Difference between an Absolute and a Limited Monarchy. A Revised Text* edited with Introduction, Notes, and Appendices *by Charles Plummer.* London: Oxford University Press, 1885. xxiii, 387pp. Reprinted 1999 by The Lawbook Exchange, Ltd. ISBN 1-886363-79-X. Cloth. $65.

Futrell, William H. *The History of American Customs Jurisprudence.* New York: Published privately, 1941. 314pp. Reprinted 1998 by The Lawbook Exchange, Ltd. LC 98-11342. ISBN 1-886363-51-X. Cloth. $60.

Greenidge, A.H.J. *The Legal Procedure of Cicero's Time.* Oxford: The Clarendon Press, 1901. xiii, 599 pp. Reprint available December 1999 by The Lawbook Exchange, Ltd. LCCN 99-26771. ISBN 1-886363-99-4. Cloth. $85.

Hale, Matthew. *The History and Analysis of the Common Law of England.* Stafford: J. Nutt, 1713. [x], 264, [28], 176 pp. Reprint available February 2000 by The Lawbook Exchange, Ltd. LCCN 99-33739. ISBN 1-58477-024-4. Cloth. $85.

Harper, Robert Francis. *The Code of Hammurabi King of Babylon. About 2250 B.C. Autographed Text transliteration...* Chicago: The University of Chicago Press, 1904. xxviii, 194, ciii (plates) pp. London: John Murray, 1832. xx, 392, lxxvi pp. Illus. LC 99-23953. ISBN 1-58477-003-1. Reprint available December 1999 by The Lawbook Exchange, Ltd. Cloth. New. $75.

Harris, Virgil M. *Ancient, Curious, and Famous Wills.* Boston: Little, Brown, and Company, 1911. xiv, 472 pp. Reprinted 1999 by The Lawbook Exchange, Ltd. LCCN 99-20588. ISBN 1-886363-93-5. Cloth. $75.

Henderson, Gerard Carl. *The Position of Foreign Corporations in American Constitutional Law. A Contribution to the History and Theory of Juristic Persons in Anglo-American Law.* Cambridge: Harvard University Press, 1918. xix, 199 pp. Reprint available November 1999 by The Lawbook Exchange, Ltd. LCCN 99-18233. ISBN 1-886363-89-7. Cloth. $50.

Holdsworth, William S. *Essays in Law and History.* Edited by A.L. Goodhart and H.G. Hanbury. Oxford: At the Clarendon Press, 1946. xv, 302 pp. Reprinted 1995 by The Lawbook Exchange, Ltd. ISBN 1-886363-13-7. Cloth. $50.

Holdsworth, W.S. *The Historians of Anglo-American Law.* New York: Columbia University Press, 1928. 175 pp. Reprinted 1994 by The Lawbook Exchange, Ltd. ISBN 0-9630106-9-7. Cloth. $50.

Johns, C.H.W. *Babylonian and Assyrian Laws, Contracts and Letters.* Edinburgh: T. & T. Clark, 1904. xxii, 424 pp. LC 99-32862. ISBN 1-58477-022-8. Reprint available December 1999 by The Lawbook Exchange, Ltd. Cloth. New. $75.

Kovalevsky, Maxime. *Modern Customs and Ancient Laws of Russia. Being the Ilchester Lectures for 1889-90.* London: David Nutt, 1891. x, 260 pp. Reprint available February 2000 by The Lawbook Exchange, Ltd. LCCN 99-16487. ISBN 1-58477-017-1. Cloth. $65.

Langdell, C.C. [1826-1906]. *A Selection of Cases on the Law of Contracts. with References and Citations. Prepared for Use as a Text-book in Harvard Law School.* Boston: Little, Brown & Co., 1871. xvi, 1022 pp. Reprinted 1999 by The Lawbook Exchange, Ltd. LCCN 99-28293. ISBN 1-58477-001-5. Cloth. $120.

[MacDonell, Sir John and Edward Manson]. *Great Jurists of the World.* Edited by Sir John MacDonell and Edward Manson. With an Introduction by Van Vechten Veeder. Boston: Little, Brown, and Company, 1914. Illustrated. xxxii, 607 pp. Reprinted 1997 by The Lawbook Exchange, Ltd. ISBN 1-886363-28-5. Cloth. $95.

Maitland, Frederick W., et.al. *A General Survey of Events, Sources, Persons & Movements in Continental Legal History. By Various European Authors.* With an introduction by Albert Kocourek. Boston: Little, Brown, 1912. liii, 754pp. Reprinted 1998 by The Lawbook Exchange, Ltd. LC 98-11159. ISBN 1-886363-47-1. Cloth. $110.

Maitland, Frederic William. *Roman Canon Law in the Church of England: Six Essays.* London: Methuen & Co., 1898. vii, 184 pp. Reprinted 1998 by The Lawbook Exchange, Ltd. LC 98-22357. ISBN 1-886363-57-9. Cloth. $65.

Maitland, Frederick W., et.al. *Select Essays in Anglo-American Legal History. By Maitland, Pollock, Holmes, Beale, Holdsworth and Others.* Boston: Little, Brown, and Company, 1907. Three volumes. 847; 823; 862 pp. Reprinted 1992 by The Lawbook Exchange, Ltd. LCCN 91-77977. ISBN 0-9630106-0-1. Cloth. $195.

Maitland, Frederick W., Montague, Francis C., *A Sketch of English Legal History.* Edited with Notes and Appendices by James F. Colby. New York: G.P. Putnam's Sons, 1915. x, 234pp. LCCN 98-11337. ISBN 1-886363-50-1. Reprinted 1998 by The Lawbook Exchange, Ltd. Cloth. $50.

Merriam, C.E., Jr. *History of the Theory of Sovereignty Since Rousseau.* New York: Columbia University Press, [1900]. x, [11]-233 pp. Reprinted 1999 by

The Lawbook Exchange, Ltd. LCCN 98-32385. ISBN 1-886363-76-5. Cloth. $65.

[Nichols, J.]. *A Collection of all the Wills, Now Known to Be Extant, of the Kings and Queens of England, Princes and Princesses of Wales, and every Branch of the Blood Royal, from the Reign of William the Conqueror, to that of Henry the Seventh Exclusive: With Explanatory Notes and a Glossary.* London: J. Nichols, 1780. x, 434 pp. Reprinted 1999 by The Lawbook Exchange, Ltd. LCCN 99-17114. ISBN 1-886363-87-0. Cloth. $75.

Ogle, Arthur. *The Canon Law in Mediaeval England. An Examination of William Lyndwood's "Provinciale," in Reply to the Late Professor F.W. Maitland.* London: John Murray, 1912. xv, 220 pp. Reprint available February 2000 by The Lawbook Exchange, Ltd. LCCN 99-33827. ISBN 1-58477-026-0. Cloth. $65.

Pollock, Sir Frederick. *The Genius of the Common Law.* New York: The Columbia University Press, 1912. vii, 141 pp. Reprint available February 2000 by The Lawbook Exchange, Ltd. LCCN 99-047160. ISBN 1-58477-043-0-1. Cloth. $55.

Pollock, Frederick and Frederic William Maitland. *The History of English Law before the Time of Edward I.* Cambridge: Cambridge University Press, 1898. Two volumes. xxxviii, 688; xiv, 691 pp. Reprinted 1996 by The Lawbook Exchange, Ltd. ISBN 1-886363-22-6. Cloth. $165.

Reeve, Tapping. [1744-1823]. *The Law of Baron and Femme, of Parent and Child, Guardian and Ward, Master and Servant, and of the Powers of the Courts of Chancery; with an Essay on the Terms Heir, Heirs, Heirs of the Body. Third Edition, With Notes and References to English and American Cases by Amasa J. Parker and Charles E. Baldwin, Counselors-At-Law.* Albany: William Gould, 1862. xlvi, 677pp. LCCN 98-36057. ISBN 1-886363-58-7. Reprinted 1998 by The Lawbook Exchange, Ltd. Cloth. $75.

Pulling, Alexander. *The Order of the Coif.* London: William Clowes & Sons, Limited, 1884. xii, 288 pp. Frontis. Illus. Reprint available February 2000 by The Lawbook Exchange, Ltd. LCCN 99-37829. ISBN 1-58477-025-2. Cloth. $95.

Sandys, Sir John Edwin. *Aristotle's Constitution of Athens. A Revised Text with an Introduction Critical and Explanatory Notes Testimonia and Indices. Second edition, Revised and Enlarged.* London: Macmillan & Co., Limited, 1902. xcii, 331 pp. Frontis. Illus. LC 99-23952. ISBN 1-58477-004-X. Reprint available March 2000 by The Lawbook Exchange, Ltd. Cloth. New. $75.

Schechter, Frank I. *The Historical Foundations of the Law Relating to Trade-Marks.* New York: Columbia University Press, 1925. xxviii, 211 pp. LC 99-41673. ISBN 1-58477-035-X. Reprint available December 1999 by The Lawbook Exchange, Ltd. Cloth. New. $60.

Schwartz, Bernard, editor. *The Code Napoleon and the Common-Law World. The Sesquicentennial Lectures Delivered at The Law Center of New York University December 13-15, 1954.* New York: New York University Press, 1956. x, 438pp. LCCN 98-34100. ISBN 1-886363-59-5. Reprinted 1998 by The Lawbook Exchange, Ltd. Cloth. $65.

Schwarz, Philip J. *Twice Condemned: Slaves and the Criminal Laws of Virginia, 1705-1865.* [Baton Rouge: Louisiana State University Press]. [1988]. xvi, 354pp. Reprinted 1998 by The Lawbook Exchange, Ltd. LCCN 98-4424 ISBN 1-886363-54-4. Cloth. $75.

Tucker, Henry St. George. *Commentaries on the Laws of Virginia. Comprising the Substance of a Course of Lectures Delivered to the Winchester Law School. With an Introduction by David Cobin and Paul Finkelman.* Richmond: Shepherd and Colin, 1846. Two volumes. 34, 468; 24, 512 pp. Reprinted 1998 by The Lawbook Exchange, Ltd. LCCN 97-10313. ISBN 1-886363-26-9. Cloth. $175.

Vinogradoff, Sir Paul. *Outlines of Historical Jurisprudence.* London: Oxford University Press, 1920. Two volumes. 428; x, 315 pp. Reprinted 1999 by The Lawbook Exchange, Ltd. LCCN 98-42298. ISBN 1-886363-64-1. Cloth. $150.

Walker, James. *The Theory of the Common Law.* Boston: Little, Brown and Co., 1852. xxiv, 130pp. Reprinted 1998 by The Lawbook Exchange, Ltd. LCCN 98-9522. ISBN 1-886363-45-5. Cloth. $65.

Warren, Charles. *History of the Harvard Law School and of Early Legal Conditions in America.* New York: Lewis Publishing Company, 1908. Three volumes. xiv, 543; iv, 560; 397 pp. Illustrated. Reprint available September 1999 by The Lawbook Exchange, Ltd. LCCN 99-29193. ISBN 1-58477-006-6. Cloth. $275.

Wiener, Leo. *Commentary to the Germanic Laws and Mediaeval Documents.* Cambridge: Harvard University Press, 1915. lxi, 224 pp. Reprint available October 1999 by The Lawbook Exchange, Ltd. LCCN 99-23969. ISBN 1-58477-005-8. Cloth. $60.

∾ Legal Reference and Bibliography ∾

Benedict, Russell. *Acts and Laws of the Thirteen Original Colonies and States: Constituting the extraordinary collection of Hon. Russell Benedict.* New York: American Art Association, 1922. [272]pp. Reprinted 1998 The Lawbook Exchange, Ltd. LCCN 98-20196 ISBN 1-886363-56-0. Cloth. $85.

Eller, Catherine Spicer. *The William Blackstone Collection in the Yale Law Library. A Bibliographical Catalogue.* New Haven: Yale University Press, 1938. Reprinted 1993 by the Lawbook Exchange, Ltd. xvii, 113 pp. Cloth. LCCN 99-38826. ISBN 0-9630106-5-4. $50.

Finkelman, Paul. *Slavery in the Courtroom. An Annotated Bibliography of American Cases.* Washington:Library of Congress, 1985. Illustrated. xxvii, 312pp. Reprinted 1998 by The Lawbook Exchange, Ltd. LCCN 98-11284. ISBN 1-886363-48-X. Cloth. $85.

Friend, William L. *Anglo-American Legal Bibliographies. An Annotated Guide.* Washington, D.C.: United States Government Printing Office, 1944. xii, 166 pp. Reprinted 1996 by The Lawbook Exchange, Ltd. ISBN 1-886363-21-8. Cloth. $65.

Hicks, Frederick. *Men and Books Famous in the Law. With an introduction by Harlan F. Stone.* Rochester, New York: Lawyers Co-operative Publishing, 1921. 259 pp. Reprinted 1992 by The Lawbook Exchange, Ltd. LCCN 92-070809. ISBN 0-9630106-2-X. Cloth.$50.

Jackson, E. Hilton. *Latin for Lawyers. Containing I: A Course in Latin, with Legal Maxims and Phrases As a Basis of Instruction. II. A Collection of Over One Thousand Latin Maxims, with English Translations, Explanatory Notes, and Cross-References. III. A Vocabulary of Latin Words.* London: Sweet & Maxwell, 1915. viii, 300 pp. Reprinted 1992 by The Lawbook Exchange, Ltd. LCCN 92-074408. ISBN 0-9630106-4-6. Cloth. $50.

McNamara, M. Frances. *Ragbag of Legal Quotations.* Albany: Matthew Bender & Company, 1960. xi, 334 pp. Reprinted 1992 by The Lawbook Exchange, Ltd. LC 92-074141. ISBN 0-9630106-3-8. Cloth. $50.

Maxwell, W. Harold and C.R. Brown. *A Complete List of British and Colonial Law Reports and Legal Periodicals. Arranged in Alphabetical and in Chronological Order with Bibliographical Notes.* **[With]:** *Check List of Canadian and Newfoundland Statutes.*[Third Edition]. Toronto: The Carswell Company, Limited, 1937. viii, 141, 49 pp. Reprinted 1995 by The Lawbook Exchange, Ltd. ISBN 1-886363-11-0. Cloth. $70.

[Worrall, John and Edward Brooke]. *Bibliotheca Legum Angliae. Or, a Catalogue of the Common and Statute Law Books of This Realm, and Some Others Relating Thereto: Giving an Account of Their Several Editions, Ancient Printers, Dates, and Prices, and Wherein They Differ. [With a Supplement to 1800]. Part I Compiled by John Worrall, Part II and Supplement Compiled by Edward Brooke. Parts I, II and Supplement bound in one volume.* London: Printed for Edward Brooke, 1788-1800. 316; 264; 48 pp. 1788-1800. Reprinted 1997 by The Lawbook Exchange, Ltd. ISBN 1-886363-29-3. Cloth. $110.

൦ Legal Sources ൦

Bouvier, John. [1787-1851]. *Institutes of American Law. New Edition by Daniel A. Gleason. In Two Volumes.* Boston:Little, Brown, & Company, 1880. Two volumes. lxviii, 651; iv, 798pp. Reprint available December 1999 by The Lawbook Exchange, Ltd. LCCN 98-54288. ISBN 1-886363-80-3. Cloth. $265.

[Cardozo, Benjamin]. *Law is Justice. Notable Opinions of Mr. Justice Cardozo.* Foreword by Robert F. Wagner. Edited by A.L. Sainer. New York: Ad Press Ltd., [1938]. xvii, 441 pp. Frontis. Reprint available September 1999 by The Lawbook Exchange, Ltd. LCCN 99-34154. ISBN 1-58477-010-4. Cloth. $75.

[Cherokee Laws]. *Compiled Laws of the Cherokee Nation.* Tahlequah, I.T.:National Advocate Print, 1881. 370pp. LC 98-12741. ISBN 1-886363-42-0. Reprinted 1998 by The Lawbook Exchange, Ltd. With a new introduction by Michael Weber. Cloth. $60.

Coke, Edward, Sir. *The First Part of the Institutes of the Laws of England, or, A commentary upon Littleton...* London, J. & W.T. Clarke, 1823. Two volumes. ccxvi,[606]; iv, [772] pp. LC 99-41675. ISBN 1-58477-033-3. Reprint available December 1999 by The Lawbook Exchange, Ltd. Cloth. New. $195.

Fortescue, John. *DeLaudibus Legum Angliae. A Treatise in Commendation of the Laws of England.* With Translation by Francis Gregor. Notes by Andrew Amos and a Life of the Author by Thomas (Fortescue) Lord Clermont. Cincinnati: Robert Clarke & Co., 1874. Reprint available September 1999 by The Lawbook Exchange, Ltd. LCCN 99-16485. ISBN 1-58477-019-8. Cloth. $65.

[St. Germain, Christopher]. [1460-1540]. *The Doctor and Student or Dialogues Between a Doctor of Divinity and a Student in the Laws of England Containing the Grounds of Those Laws Together with Questions and Cases Concerning the Equity*

Thereof Revised and Corrected by William Muchall, Gent. to which are added two pieces concerning Suits in Chancery by Subpoena. Cincinnati:Robert Clarke & Co., 1874. xiv, 401pp. Reprinted 1998 by The Lawbook Exchange, Ltd. LCCN 98-11338. ISBN 1-886363-49-8. Cloth. $65.

Woodbine, George E. *Four Thirteenth Century Law Tracts. A Thesis Presented to the Faculty of the Graduate Schol of Yale University in Candidacy for the Degree of Doctor of Philosophy.* New Haven: Yale University Press, 1910. vi, 183 pp. Reprint available October 1999 by The Lawbook Exchange, Ltd. LCCN 99-29294. ISBN 1-58477-007-4. Cloth. $50.

☙ *Legal Treatises* ☙

Beck, Theodric Romeyn. *Elements of Medical Jurisprudence.* Albany: Websters and Skinners, 1823. Two volumes. xxxiv, 418; viii, [9]-471 pp. Reprinted 1997 by The Lawbook Exchange, Ltd. ISBN 1-886363-24-2. Cloth. $125.

Calabresi, Guido. *A Common Law for the Age of Statutes.* Cambridge: Harvard University Press, 1982. xi, 319 pp. LC 99-44889. ISBN 1-58477-040-6. Reprint available December 1999 by The Lawbook Exchange, Ltd. Cloth. New. $85.

Freeman, A.C. *A Treatise of the Law of Judgments. Including All Final Determinations of the Rights of Parties in Actions or Proceedings at Law or in Equity. Revised, and Greatly Enlarged by Edward W. Tuttle.* San Francisco: Bancroft-Whitney, 1925. Three volumes. 1216; 1280; 1264 pp. Reprinted 1993 by The Lawbook Exchange, Ltd. ISBN 0-9630106-6-2. Cloth. $295.

Gilmore, Grant. *Security Interests in Personal Property.* Boston: Little, Brown & Company, 1965. Two volumes. xxxiv, 651; xiii, 653-1508 pp. Reprinted 1999 by The Lawbook Exchange, Ltd. LCCN 99-10258. ISBN 1-886363-81-1. Cloth. $195.

Pomeroy, John N. *A Treatise on Equity Jurisprudence As Administered in the United States of America. Adapted for All the States and to the Union of Legal and Equitable Remedies under the Reformed Procedure.* San Francisco and New York: Bancroft-Whitney and Lawyers Cooperative, 1941. Five volumes. 914; 1134; 1063; 1104; 716 pp. Reprinted 1995 by The Lawbook Exchange, Ltd. ISBN 1-886363-05-6. Cloth. $450.

Pothier, Robert Joseph [1699-1772]. *A Treatise on Obligations, Considered in a Moral and Legal View. Translated from the French of Pothier. Translated by Francois-Xavier Martin.* Newburn, N.C.: Martin & Ogden, 1802. Reprint available December 1999 by The Lawbook Exchange, Ltd. With a new introduction by Warren M. Billings. LC 98-38360. ISBN 1-886363-62-5. Cloth. $75.

Pothier, R.J. *Treatise on the Contract of Sale.* Translated from the French by L.S. Cushing. Boston: Charles C. Little and James Brown, 1889. xvi, 406 pp. LC 99-10260. ISBN 1-886363-82-X. Reprint available December 1999 by The Lawbook Exchange, Ltd. Cloth. New. $70.

[Ricardo, David]. McCulloch, J.R. *The Works of David Ricardo, Esq., M.P. with a Notice of the Life and Writings of the Author.* London: John Murray, 1846. xxxiii, 584 pp. LC 99-39612. ISBN 1-58477-028-7. Reprint available March 2000 by The Lawbook Exchange, Ltd. Cloth. New. $90.

Sears, John H. *Trust Estates as Business Companies. [Second Edition].* Kansas City, Mo.:Vernon Law Book Company, 1921. xx, 782 pp. [1921]. Reprinted June 1998 by The Lawbook Exchange, Ltd. LCCN 97-32423 ISBN 1-886363-41-2. Cloth. $95.

❧ Philosophy of Law ❧

Austin, John. *The Province of Jurisprudence Determined.* London: John Murray, 1832. xx, 392, lxxvi pp. LC 99-33457. ISBN 1-58477-023-6. Reprint available December 1999 by The Lawbook Exchange, Ltd. Cloth. New. $75.

Fuller, Lon L. *The Law in Quest of Itself.* Boston: Beacon Press, 1966. [vi], 150 pp. Reprint available October 1999 by The Lawbook Exchange, Ltd. LCCN 99-32863. ISBN 1-58477-016-3. Cloth. $45.

Jhering, Rudolf Von. *Law as a Means to an End.* Translated from the German by Isaac Husik with an Editorial Preface by Joseph H. Drake and with Introductions by Henry Lamm and W.M. Geldart. Boston: The Boston Book Company, 1913. lxi, 483 pp. Reprinted 1999 by The Lawbook Exchange, Ltd. LCCN 99-23754. ISBN 1-58477-009-0. Cloth. $80.

Jhering, Rudolph von. *The Struggle for Law. Translated from the Fifth German Edition by John J. Lalor. Second Edition, with an Introduction by Albert Kocourek.* Chicago: Callaghan and Company, 1915. lii, 138 pp. Reprinted 1997 by The Lawbook Exchange, Ltd. ISBN 1-886363-25-0. Cloth. $60.

Kelsen, Hans. [1881-1973]. *General Theory of Law and State.* Translated by Anders Wedberg. Cambridge: Harvard University Press, 1945. xxxiii, 516pp.

LCCN 98-32334. ISBN 1-886363-74-9. Reprinted 1999 by The Lawbook Exchange, Ltd. Cloth. $75.

Pollock, Sir Frederick. *The Genius of the Common Law.* New York: The Columbia University Press, 1912. vii, 141 pp. Reprint available February 2000 by The Lawbook Exchange, Ltd. LCCN 99-047160. ISBN 1-58477-043-0-1. Cloth. $55.

Radin, Max. *Law as Logic and Experience.* New Haven: Yale University Press, 1940. ix, [1], 171 pp. Reprint available February 2000 by The Lawbook Exchange, Ltd. LCCN 99-30670. ISBN 1-58477-008-2. Cloth. $55.

Vinogradoff, Paul. *Custom and Right.* Oslo: H. Aschehoug, 1925. 110 pp. LC 99-0474851. ISBN 1-58477-048-1. Reprint available March 2000 by The Lawbook Exchange, Ltd. Cloth. New. $45.

◌ Special Editions◌

Stokes, I.N. Phelps. *The Iconography of Manhattan Island 1498-1909.* New York: Robert H. Dodd, 1915. Six volumes. Reprinted 1998 by The Lawbook Exchange, Ltd. LCCN 97-30604. ISBN 1-886363-30-7. Cloth. $750.

◌ U.S. Constitutional History ◌

Bauer, Elizabeth Kelley. *Commentaries on the Constitution 1790-1860.* New York: Columbia University Press, 1952. 400 pp. Reprinted 1999 by The Lawbook Exchange, Ltd. LCCN 98-45409. ISBN 1-886363-66-8. Cloth. $75.

Beard, Charles A. *The Supreme Court and the Constitution.* New York: The Macmillan Company, 1912. vii, 127 pp. Reprinted 1999 by The Lawbook Exchange, Ltd. LCCN 98-50368. ISBN 1-886363-78-1. Cloth. $45.

Bondy, William. *Separation of Governmental Powers in History, in Theory, and in the Constitutions.* New York: Columbia College, 1896. Reprinted 1999 by The Lawbook Exchange, Ltd. vi,[7]-185, [1] pp. LCCN 98-44994. ISBN 1-886363-65-X. Cloth. $65.

Cohn, Morris M. *An Introduction to the Study of the Constitution; A Study showing the play of Physical and Social Factors in the Creation of Institutional Law.* Baltimore: The Johns Hopkins Press, 1892. xi, 235 pp. LC 99-38730. ISBN

1-58477-032-5. Reprint available March 2000 by The Lawbook Exchange, Ltd. Cloth. New. $50.

Cooley, Thomas McIntyre. *A Treatise on the Constitutional Limitations Which Rest Upon the Legislative Power of the States of the American Union. [1st edition].* Boston: Little, Brown, and Co., 1868. xlvii, 720pp. Reprinted 1999 by The Lawbook Exchange, Ltd. LCCN 99-20589. ISBN 1-886363-92-7. Cloth. $95.

Cooley, Thomas M. *A Treatise on the Constitutional Limitations which Rest Upon the Legislative Power of the States of the American Union. Fifth edition.* Boston: Little, Brown, and Co., 1883. lxxxi, 886pp. Reprinted October 1998 by The Lawbook Exchange, Ltd. LCCN 98-12730. ISBN 1-886363-53-6. Cloth. $120.

Dodd, Walter Fairleigh. *The Revision and Amendment of State Constitutions.* Baltimore: The Johns Hopkins Press, 1910. xvii, 350 pp. Reprinted 1999 by The Lawbook Exchange, Ltd. ISBN 1-886363-73-0. Cloth. $65.

Duer, William Alexander. *A Course of Lectures on the Constitutional Jurisprudence of the United States; Delivered Annually in Columbia College, New York. The Second Edition, Revised, Enlarged, and Adapted to Professional as well as General Use.* Boston: Little, Brown & Co., 1856. xxiv, 545 pp. LC 99-16385. ISBN 1-58477-020-1. Reprint available December 1999 by The Lawbook Exchange, Ltd. Cloth. New. $85.

Fisher, Sydney George. *The Evolution of the Constitution of the United States. Showing That It Is a Development of Progressive History and Not an Isolated Document Struck Off at a Given Time or an Imitation of English or Dutch Forms of Government.* Philadelphia: J.B. Lippincott, 1897. 398 pp. Reprinted 1996 by The Lawbook Exchange, Ltd. LCCN 97-41054. ISBN 1-886363-08-0. Cloth. $65.

Flanders, Henry. *An Exposition of the Constitution of the United States. Designed as a Manual of Instruction.* Philadelphia: E.H. Butler & Co., 1860. xii, 311 pp. Reprint available October 1999 by The Lawbook Exchange, Ltd. LCCN 99-31594. ISBN 1-58477-014-7. Cloth. $60.

Ford, Paul Leicester. *Pamphlets on the Constitution of the United States, Published During Its Discussion by the People 1787-1788.* Brooklyn, N.Y., 1888. viii, 451 pp. LC 99-25089. ISBN 1-886363-95-1. Reprint available March 2000 by The Lawbook Exchange, Ltd. Cloth. New. $75.

Holt, W. Stull. *Treaties Defeated by the Senate. A Study of the Struggle Between President and Senate Over the Conduct of Foreign Relations.* Baltimore: The Johns Hopkins Press, 1933. vi, [1],328 pp. Reprint available February 2000 by The

Lawbook Exchange, Ltd. LCCN 99-39606. ISBN 1-58477-029-5. Cloth. $65.

[Madison, James]. Hunt, Gaillard, Scott, James Brown. *The Debates in The Federal Convention of 1787 Which Framed the Constitution of the United States of America.* New York: Oxford University Press, 1920. xcvii, [1], 731 pp. Reprinted 1999 by The Lawbook Exchange, Ltd. LCCN 98-51911. ISBN 1-886363-77-3. Cloth. $110.

Minor, Raleigh C. *Notes on the Science of Government and the Relations of the States to the United States.* [Charlottesville]: University of Virginia, 1913. x, 171 pp. Reprinted 1995 by The Lawbook Exchange,Ltd. ISBN 1-886363-09-9. Cloth. $40.

Story, Joseph. [1779-1845]. *A Familiar Exposition of the Constitution of the United States: Containing a Brief Commentary on Every Clause, Explaining the True Nature, reasons, and Objects Thereof; Designed for the Use of School, Libraries and General Readers. With an Appendix, Containing Important Public Documents, Illustrative of the Constitution.* New York: Harper & Brothers: 1865. 372 pp. Reprinted 1999 by The Lawbook Exchange, Ltd. ISBN 1-886363-71-4. Cloth. $60.

[Taylor, John]. [1753-1824]. *A Defence of the Measures of the Administration of Thomas Jefferson. By Curtius.* Washington: Samuel H. Smith, 1804. 136 pp. Reprinted 1999 by The Lawbook Exchange, Ltd. LCCN 99-24139. ISBN 1-886363-97-8. Cloth. $60.

Taylor, John. *Construction Construed and Constitutions Vindicated.* Richmond:printed by Shepherd & Pollard, 1820. iv, 344pp. Reprinted 1998 by The Lawbook Exchange, Ltd. LCCN 97-49411. ISBN 1-886363-43-9. Cloth. $65.

Taylor, John. *An Inquiry into the Principles and Policy of the Government of the United States.* Fredericksburg:Green and Cady, 1814. With an introduction by Roy Franklin Nichols, Yale University Press, 1950. 562pp. Reprinted 1998 by The Lawbook Exchange, Ltd. LCCN 98-11147. ISBN 1-886363-46-3. Cloth. $75.

Tucker, Henry St. George. *Limitations on the Treaty-Making Power Under the Constitution of the United States.* Boston: Little, Brown, and Company, 1915. xxi, 444 pp. Reprint available February 2000 by The Lawbook Exchange, Ltd. LCCN 99-31589. ISBN 1-58477-015-5. Cloth. $75.

Tucker, St. George. *Blackstone's Commentaries. With Notes of Reference to the Constitution and Laws, of the Federal Government of the United States, and of the Commonwealth of Virginia. In Five Volumes, with an Appendix to Each volume,*

Containing Short Tracts upon Such Subjects As Appeared Necessary to Form a Connected View of the Laws of Virginia As a Member of the Federal Union. Philadelphia: William Young Birch and Abraham Small, 1803. Five volumes. Reprinted 1996 by The Lawbook Exchange, Ltd. ISBN 1-886363-15-3. Cloth. $450.

[Upshur, Abel Parker]. *A Brief Enquiry Into the True Nature and Character of Our Federal Government, being a review of Judge Story's Commentaries on the Constitution of the United States. By a Virginian.* Petersburg: Printed by Edmund and Julian C. Ruffin, 1840. 132pp. Reprinted 1998 by The Lawbook Exchange, Ltd. LCCN 97-11151. ISBN 1-886363-44-7. Cloth. $45.

Wright, John S. *Citizenship Sovereignty.* Chicago: Published for American Citizens, the True Maintainers of State Sovereignty, 1864. Reprinted 1998 by The Lawbook Exchange, Ltd. LCCN 98-15940 ISBN 1-886363-55-2. Cloth. $65.